Brothers & Sisters
Like These

An Anthology of Writing by Veterans

BROTHERS & SISTERS LIKE THESE

AN ANTHOLOGY OF WRITING BY VETERANS

REDHAWK
PUBLICATIONS

Redhawk Publications
The Catawba Valley Community College Press
2550 US Hwy 70 SE
Hickory, NC 28602

ISBN: 978-1-959346-00-5

Library of Congress Number applied for.

Printed in the United States of America

redhawkpublications.com

Table of Contents

Preface by Dr. Bruce Kelly, MD.

This is a story about stories ... a prelude to the deeply felt expressions in the pages that follow.

Writing programs for veterans have existed since the Second World War to help veterans make sense of their military experience and honor the voices inside needing to be heard.

Quoting Ron Capps of the Veterans Writing Project, "Not everyone is a story teller, but everyone has a story to tell." He reminds us that for veterans with PTSD, "either you control the memory or the memory controls you."

I came to the VA as a Primary Care physician in 2011 knowing little about military culture, and nothing of the experience of combat. It didn't take long to realize how many of the Vietnam veterans in my care were still carrying wounds from their time in country. It was hard to accept they were but a fraction of the estimated 250,000 Vietnam veterans living with PTSD five decades later.

They told me what war had done to their emotions, behaviors, sleep, dreams, and moods ... to relationships with family, friends, careers ... about avoidance and addictions ... how it was still hard to go out in public, to have normal conversations ... to trust that this was a world where they could feel safe, could love, and be loved.

They told me about battles fought, comrades lost, regrets they couldn't shake ... about anger at being on the losing end of a war despite winning all the battles. They spoke to their treatment on returning home, and the shame and rage triggered by an ungrateful nation that sent them to serve on its behalf.

I came to learn about moral injury, defined as "extreme guilt and shame from something done or witnessed that goes against one's values".

I wondered why it would ever surprise us that sending moral individuals to a world defined by death and destruction would lead to emotions coming unglued, to neurons going awry. I wondered how anyone could come through unscathed, and came to understand that few really did.

As I listened to these veterans the unseen wounds were up close and personal, sitting next to me … the men often avoiding eye contact, their voices cracking, often holding back tears. They seemed afraid to speak what was on their minds, rightfully feeling they'd been abandoned to carry their wounds alone, with little hope for anything beyond the reality they'd been forced to live.

I came to better understand the weight of burdens carried, each in their own way but with so many common threads. Most out of some necessity had buried what they carried, having no way to reconcile or leave the war behind.

Gratefully I came to know of former North Carolina Poet Laureate Joseph Bathanti, a Professor at Appalachian State University. Joseph as his signature project spent two years leading writing workshops for veterans across the state. He understood as I the importance of veterans being able to tell their stories in a safe, non-judgmental setting. We both believed the work had the potential to help heal what remained wounded.

In 2014, with the blessing of our medical center's leadership, grants from the North Carolina Arts and North Carolina Humanities Councils, and support from the community, Professor Bathanti was named Writer-in-Residence at Charles George. We eagerly began planning a creative writing program that we hoped would restore a sense of these veterans' humanity, and in so doing, foster a degree of recovery.

As I recruited men during routine medical visits, I began to see more deeply how remarkable each of them were, all heroes in their own right who needed to unburden themselves in ways they may or may not had yet recognized.

They told me they were reluctant to bring the war back up, that creative writing or poetry seemed like a "cockamamie idea." that they couldn't write, had trouble with spelling, bad experiences with groups, and more. But they too gradually spoke more about the wounds that haunted them and were often ready to try anything that might help.

Thanks to the ongoing Charles George grant and community

support, we held four eight-week sessions over the next few years involving 38 veterans. We continued to meet monthly with 25 of them. These burgeoning writers served as the catalysts and mentors for the remarkable work yet to come. The pages to follow are but a fraction of the stories now told over the past eight years.

Our time together wasn't always easy. There were difficult sessions. Not all the men chose to continue. There were often tears of some kind for all of us. Mine came often hearing the pain they felt, from the deep respect I held for their stories, and from overwhelming gratitude watching their healing unfold. For many of the men it was transformative in ways we never could have imagined.

Though we didn't see their courage in country, we saw it over and over in Classroom B. Their commitment, honesty, and writing took our breath away again and again. It often felt like church from the work of the soul they engaged in, and the deep reverence we communally felt for their service, sacrifice, and for one another.

The men found an ability to articulate memories, losses, and triumphs in their own unique voices. We watched a sense of brotherhood evolve, and witnessed the men begin to reclaim the humanity taken from them in an increasingly forgotten war.

In August 2016, 18 of the veterans agreed to participate in a staged reading at Asheville Community Theater titled Brothers Like These. We shortly thereafter did a second at Appalachian State to a standing room only crowd of students and teachers, and the following year a third, again at the community theatre. These launched another 10 readings across North Carolina over the next few years.

On each occasion the audience was deeply touched, frequently in tears but always leaving with a new understanding and respect for all who served in Vietnam, and by proxy in combat zones wherever they may be. The men felt honored, empowered, and a long overdue sense they were indeed heroes of their own stories. The readings provided a platform for the welcome home they never received.

A chapbook of the same name provided a visible reminder of their commitment, and the stories they had to tell. It remains St. Andrews

Press' all-time best seller.

Two additional groups, VA Innovation Network funding, and a Mini-documentary sponsored by the Healthy US Collaborative allowed us to spread the work and advocacy even further.

And now to these 77 remarkable stories you hold in your hands.

Core members of the group, transformed by their healing experience, formed a non-profit to continue the work outside the VA, The North Carolina Veterans Writing Alliance. They from the start made it a priority to expand the work to post-911 and women veterans, evolving into Brothers and Sisters Like These.

Our veterans from the post-911 wars know their own horrors and losses. Their sacrifices and struggles are no less daunting, their need to be heard no less critical. The Writing Alliance's commitment to recognize and honor their younger brethren holds equal moral imperative. These stories too need to be told, and heard.

The accomplishments of this band of brothers and sisters are astonishing. Each gathering, each conversation, each story told over the past several years have led to this additional volume of stories.

The Alliance has continued to hold writing groups under the direction of award-winning writer Elizabeth Heaney, with veteran writers themselves helping lead the groups. They've continued to do public readings at libraries, schools, Memorial and Veteran's Days, Honor Flights, and the Flat Rock Playhouse among others. They've brought song writers from Nashville to create music based on their stories. They've held multiple performances with the Black Box Dance Theater.

Maybe most importantly they've continued to give voice to the next generation of men and women who've experienced the traumas of combat in service to our nation. They've brought together veterans from different eras to share and heal together.

They've brought together family members to join them as their voices too hold deep meaning. Quoting Ron Capps again, "No one goes to war alone." Those left behind pay a deep price, often for decades to come. They much too often share in the burdens of war, including the ultimate sacrifice.

They bring you here a collection of stories that will inform and bring you to a deeper understanding and appreciation for the service and sacrifice of not only these veterans and family members, but by proxy all who have known war. You'll see up close and personal the depth of feeling and creativity that resides in the human spirit despite what traumas it's experienced.

Words and relationships have the ability to build shared community, and through those, to help heal. We welcome you to this vibrant, growing community of the ties that bind.

To quote the poet Muriel Rukeyser, 'The universe is not made up of atoms, it's made up of stories."

I hope you're as moved and inspired as I in the reading. Open your hearts, feel deeply, and join us in welcoming home the next and every veteran you meet, now and forever.

Dr. Richard Kelly, MD
Asheville VA Medical Center

Introduction by Elizabeth Heaney, MA LPC.

The stories you're about to read had a long journey before they landed in this book, and I want you to know how they arrived here, because that journey matters.

Imagine a meeting room (at a church, a library, a hospital basement, a VFW post), with several conference-room tables arranged in a square with folding chairs pulled up around the outside edge. Wary folks file in and take a seat, darting glances at each other. Some know the jungles of Vietnam or the Ben Wah valley, others know Kandahar or the sandstorms of Iraq; some know the raw power of the high seas, others know the tense precision of landing helicopters while under enemy fire. They're unsure of what they're doing in that meeting room, some of them questioning whether they should have come to this veterans' writing class at all. Many of these veterans haven't gathered with other veterans since their days of service; most have never done any writing. In fact, most have never told their stories before – not to their wives, their children, their parents, siblings or friends. They've kept those memories shut away because they were told to do so, or because they thought no one was interested, or because they had tried at some point in time to speak up . . . and all they got was a blank stare, a puzzled look or a look of mild disdain. Some have crossed paths with a few veterans over the years, and stories might have been swapped. But nothing like this writing group.

So, this meeting room with tables and chairs? It isn't a familiar setting and this whole writing thing seems a strange project to be a part of. If you were there, you'd hear mumbled comments like, "I've never done anything like this before." Or "I'm not sure how this writing stuff is going to help anything." There's some awkward shifting around in their seats and a strained silence before the class begins. They spend the moments fiddling with pens, shuffling paper, waiting for the start-time to arrive, unsure what to expect.

What brought them here? Down the road (a few classes into the process), they sometimes confess to having a desire to unburden, to share, to see if others have carried the same weight; they talk about a need to 'come home' more completely, and a realization that it's time to reckon with all they've carried inside. Others want the camaraderie, having spent decades in isolation – emotional isolation for some, and pretty thorough physical isolation for others. They've spent so many years avoiding the memories, the fears, the hurt and the losses.

Around those tables there's officers and enlisted, from all branches of service; men and women; veterans from multiple deployments or no deployments at all; those who've carried their stories for several long decades (more than fifty years), and those who've carried them a shorter while. Every single person here knows the price of service, knows so much about sacrifice, knows about loss of innocence and the complicated journey of love-of-country and love of the brothers and sisters who serve next to you. Their stories matter . . .

We get them writing as soon as possible. Prompts are offered "Write about _____" (something like "leaving" or "coming home" or "mission"). They put pen to page and the stories start to pour through – slowly at first, quick takes on different aspects of their military years – but there's a quiet depth to the stories, too. Sometimes, they simply write a list of details or events; that's as much as they can put together. Others write and write and write and have a hard time stopping the words when the time for writing is up.

When asked if they want to read that first bit of writing, there's more awkward silence. They look around the room or stare at the floor, not sure what to do with that invitation – pages shuffled, pens twirled, nobody moves. Finally, one person raises their hand, reads what they wrote, and hears the group's responses. Then another does the same. And another. They start to get the rhythm of writing then sharing, reading then listening, remembering and 'going there' with each other. In "going there," they witness each other's long journey, they nod with understanding at how hard it is to truly come home. They get quiet and pay such close, sincere attention while the first few veterans read, and they start to see how meaningful it might be to share the stories with each other.

During the second class, hands go up so fast we start a list for who will read next. There are tears or laughter, common ground, head-nods, heartbreaking memories and eyes-closed-in-remembrance. Sometimes, they share language – shorthand phrases, acronyms, remembered-nicknames, the names of villages, mountain ranges or LZ's. Sometimes, they share losses – a buddy, a way of life, an ease in themselves they've never regained. They chuckle at shared jokes and tease each other about the branch of service they were in or their MOS (military job). They're able to relate to each other in the most nuanced, sincere, emotional way.

By the third week, they stay a bit after class. They gather in small groups, asking each other questions and remembering that awful enemy-assault or that funny incident in basic. The clock ticks, but they've stopped watching the time; they're lost in finding connection. They huddle together, laughing and then sometimes reaching out a hand to touch a classmate's shoulder – that early awkwardness melted in the lovely 'heat' of stories that don't flinch from blazing truth.

Week after week, the bonds strengthen and deepen. Stories become more poignant, sometimes almost unbearably frank and full of painful remembrance or complex confusion. But the laughter is there, too.

They remember the bonds they shared with others they served with, and they truly become "brothers and sisters" again. They want to hear each other's stories and while they realize their own stories will be heard (finally), they also know their buddies carry similar stories deserving to be heard. They show up week after week, drenched in quiet courage, eager for this journey of writing.

Later, they say the writing helps free their memories, their relationships, and their hearts. They say they feel more alive again – some marvel because they never thought they could feel free of those wildly-heavy memories of combat or service. Others, having broken down while sharing their stories, find new freedom and begin to imagine letting go of all they've carried.

It's a privilege to share their stories with you. You can be sure it cost each of them a heavy price to live these stories, and it wasn't a simple process to write them down – but sharing them with you is an extraordinary offering from these veterans. I hope their stories touch your hearts as profoundly as they have touched mine.

November 11, 2022

Elizabeth Heaney, MA LPC
Writer-in-Residence, North Carolina Veterans Writing Alliance, Author of *The Honor Was Mine: A Look Inside the Struggles of Military Veterans*

A Good Place by Mike Smith

"It's against the rules," he said. "I can't let anybody use a ladder for the high ones."

My strength was gone, broken down in the simple process of arrival. Now there were rules.

I looked into the park ranger's eyes and stood motionless as my anger rose. I dove into the quiet inner pool where I deluded myself that nothing mattered. My tears stopped. For a moment, I didn't hear him. I just saw his face and watched his lips move. I glanced toward the Wall. They were there. The fluttering of their words and cries beat against me until things came back into focus.

"Hey, friend," he said. "I said I can't point out the ladder to you." He gestured toward a ten-foot aluminum ladder lying in the grass a few yards away. "I'm going way over there to help somebody I just now saw. I'll be pretty far away from that ladder I didn't point out." He handed me a slip of paper and a rubbing pencil. The paper said "Vietnam Veterans Memorial" across the top. In kindness and understanding, he walked away.

Shaking hit me as I climbed. Larry's name swam toward me through returning tears. I didn't know if I could hold the paper still.

Silence again as I reached toward Larry. When I smoothed the paper against granite, the bright air and bustle of the crowd faded away completely. I watched someone carry Larry toward me behind the hard stone, pressing him tight behind the polished surface. The name rose clearly onto the paper as I rubbed the pencil back and forth. When I reached the "H" in "CHRISTMAN," I looked at the face of the soldier carrying Larry. It was Tex. He was dressed for rifle team, steel helmet cocked back, showing red hair and freckles. He smiled childishly at me even though I had missed when I reached for him so long ago, and he was here even though I had forgotten. He was smiling at me, and I had been angry with him for dying. I remembered the tight bond when the war reached out to consume us. I rubbed Larry's name onto paper, and

I was forgiven.

Now I recalled Tex, his face, his life, his death. I wrapped my arms around the ladder and held on. Holding, I watched Tex walk with Larry in his arms back into the deep polished black, smiling back at me, smiling and receding into the ocean of granite until all that was left was my reflection. I climbed down the ladder, dropped to my knees and wept, holding onto the second rung to keep from curling up on the cold stones.

Afterwards, I walked. At the far end of the Wall near the statue of three soldiers, I saw a woman kneeling, struggling to take a rubbing with a thin pencil. I handed her the rubbing pencil. She looked up and asked, "Did you lose anyone?"

I looked back down the long expanse of shortened lives. I wanted to walk away, but she stood up and put her arms around me.

I wished Tex had lived to feel her arms. In her touch, it was okay to be alive; the warmth of a living, caring person brought me back. I stood in her arms holding Larry's etched existence, remembering Tex. It was a good place to be.

The Gift by Stacie Litsenberger

In September 2005, the US Army was going out into the rural areas of Iraq and conducting humanitarian missions. These were called MEDCAP missions and conducted by the Battalion aid station and civil affairs unit. I was invited along, as the units knew me as an Occupational Therapist in the Combat Stress Detachment and my work at the Combat Support Hospital (CSH).

My mission as an OT was to fit a 12-year-old boy with polio in a wheelchair. His dad was asking for surgery to fix him and our team explained this was not possible and why. In these rural villages, the citizens had no real knowledge of medical issues. I did the wheelchair fitting and taught the father how to transfer him. For 12 years, this young boy had been carried everywhere by his father.

I asked our leadership if I could wander around the outside of the large home to look around. I was given permission and started taking pictures of the children playing outside and of the village gathering to catch a glimpse of us. We were quite a sight with our HUMMVs all locked and loaded with 50 caliber weapons, guards, and a team of devoted medical providers and other professionals ready to provide a day of full medical assistance. I was dressed in full battle rattle consisting of a helmet, my protective vest, M-16, and a full combat load of ammo. It was at least 125 degrees, and I was soaking wet with sweat. Soon, the group of gathered Iraqi women motioned to me to come over to them and next I was welcomed into the kitchen/common area. They were so interested in me.

Once seated inside, they motioned to take my camera and they looked it over and started taking pictures. I imagine they hadn't ever seen or used a digital camera before. Then, true to the middle-eastern tradition, they started to want to give me all kinds of items. They were super curious if I was really a female—fortunately they did not want proof. I figured I could give them answers to their questions and left to get the male Iraqi translator. I asked him if he could go into their living area and he said yes. While with the women, we answered all of their

questions and I left with only one gift. As we left the room, the translator kept saying "thank you" over and over again in Arabic. I finally asked
him why. He explained how as an Iraqi male, he was never allowed in
the women's area. However, with me he was seen as a translator and
could assist me. He was so pleased. I joined my Army team to eat at a big
plastic white table and chairs. Our guards came in to take quick turns
to eat and were grateful for a few minutes out of all their heavy, hot gear.
The meal was a traditional middle eastern meal, an entire cooked lamb
with rice on huge platters. The Iraqi men served us by grabbing huge
fistfuls of food and literally dumped it on our plates. While we ate, they
masterfully grabbed more food and threw it again onto our plates. There
was no saying "no."

I had rice in my hair from the flying food and as they broke the
lamb apart - the grease would splatter into our faces. We were all laughing. Once we were completely full, the Iraqi men sat on the floor to eat
their meal. As we left for the day, I enjoyed my role as helping a young
child become more independent and meeting the Iraqi women and girls.
I hoped that coming to the village would inspire the girls to dream for
more. To see firsthand how women serve proudly in the US military
and sit with the men.

Oh, and the gift. It was a really ornate bra. :)

What I Carried by Dean Little

Each morning after, I tossed into a pile,
blood-stiff fatigue pants, plated like armor,
fatigue jacket with splattered red splotches,
echoing screams in silence, in memory
I would not carry them starting this day.
In the morning thumping, like war drums
artillery fire continues from the night,
war knows not rest, nor sleep.

Each day I scrub clean,
shed the red dust, bits of flesh.
Drag a razor over boyish man whiskers.
Grab clean, or near clean,
fatigues, skivvies, socks; brush
red shit or just shit off my boots,
maybe make a smile in the mirror
to see if that part still works.

I move through the hooch collecting up
the squad I am responsible for each day,
move them to where we stand in line,
officers and NCOs give news, orders, warnings,
squawk, squawk, yeah, yeah, get it done.
Into the mess, grease served by air,
small white worms moving in grits today.
Cook says he'll reheat until movement stops.
Friends join for talk or in silence.
Sarah is in Officer's country,
sipping her coffee, stealing glances at me,
telegraphing a night's stolen moments, stop.
I am tired, intimacy worth the fatigue.

First the team herds itself together, reports
given on our charges, new, recovering, the dead.
I walk to start my assignments,
strap on stainless steel scissions and hemostats.
Trays of needles and slides, malaria sticks and
blood draws, IV starts, tubes for front, back, sides.
Sometimes carry restraints for the delirious or mad,
carrying the sadness and lost hope in their eyes.

Radioman's bad news box shouts casualties:
a lot. Some are children, some are women.
We treat civilians too, to win hearts and minds.
All wards cut loose responders to receiving,
we grab our steel, our large bores, and tourniquets,
we are ready to strip with shear edges but first
we assemble on the helipad carrying liters and
gurneys to unload choppers and ferry wounded inside.
We sort by triage at the door, first come first on stretchers
held up by sawhorses, like a construction site or a
site of destruction or of sanity's deconstruction.
Not enough room? Use the floor, the hallway,
avoid the morgue. Avoid the morgue.
Clamp the pumpers, sew the parts into opposition,
prep for surgery, hold parts on during x-rays. Stick them,
tube them, bandages press and hold, tape well.

Carry the expectant to a second place,
quieter and less busy, lights are softer.
We carry pain killers for comfort,
we carry blankets for the shock-shivering ones,
we take turns rotating to the goodbye place.
Our hands drift out to wipe blood from eyes and faces.
I see the nine-year-old's angelic face in repose,

he could be sleeping; I wish it were quieter.
Tasked to take his vitals every fifteen minutes
until he lets go, until he meets his eternity,
I move around to grab a pulse from his neck,
and then, and then I see the punched-out hole,
rectangular, seared by metal fragment, deep.
His wound is not prepped, his little boy soft
black hair tries to cover the bad thing.

A place is found for all, some helicoptered out.
Surgery lists create a stretcher queue to the OR.
The air is redolent with the smell of copper,
sweat, urine, excrement, unspeakable things.
Receiving is decorated with IV bottles, tubing,
bandages draped across bodies, battle dressing
overflowing cans, red and green fatigue rags
wrapped like bunting round the sawhorse legs,
as if we had feverishly prepared it for,
a macabre 'Festival of Death.'

Knowing our invitation to casualty care,
is a given and will be given repeatedly,
we are released to our other duties.
My daily interviews with our mentally injured
reveal a dark panoply of horror stories,
lamentations of lost friends dragging their entrails,
Wait, I just saw the rest of the story.
So, I document what I have learned but the horror
does not flow to paper, it is not expunged,
it stays, it stains, I carried it then
and I carry it now.

Every couple, every several days, during
raining sideways monsoons or the hot dry,

it was my turn for the perimeter defense force.
My turn to draw and carry my M16, flak jacket,
steel pot, a droopy fourteen magazine bandolier,
a canteen and three flares for use if needed.
Climb a tower on the line, spend twelve hours
watching, scanning in fifty-yard arcs. Waiting.

Carrying fatigue was a constant state of being.
Working twelve to fourteen hour shifts six days
or more. Pulling perimeter guard, heading up
supplies to two orphanages, out of pocket,
by midnight requisition or ten finger appropriation
Medcap with the marines, lose another half day
of sleep, precious sleep, off my feet, stopped.
Whittling away my one hundred sixty-eight hours,
leaving few for s**t, shower, shave, writing letters,
friendship and of course, Sarah, for a while.

"There's something happening here
But what it is ain't exactly clear ...
Everybody look what's going down"
69-70 were troubled times In Vietnam, -
in many ways, bad for morale, rising
racial animosity, it simmered, it flared
sometimes it exploded, riots, fragging.
Mostly in the rear where your life was
not so dependent on that man
over there you've learned to call brother.
Some needed people to hate. Some of us,
who cared about the stranger,
were called 'gook lovers.'
There were days when I felt apart,
separated and segregated,
threatened with harm, with death for

carrying the burden of compassion.
Isolated from those who found it easy,
easier to hate so many for what
few had done. I carried anger too, for
having to watch forward for one enemy
and having to watch my back, for another.

Mostly, I carried a growing sense of running
out of time. Three times I carried requests
to move to a line or medevac unit,
Each time my colonel told personnel
I will give you two medics but not him.
No bulls**t, I had worked too hard, done
too much, was too worthy to transfer.
I was short, I gave up trying.
I had closed the eyes of my brothers,
closed the eyes of women and children.
I saw so much valor and sacrifice
by those who endured the brunt of combat.
I saw so many times the efforts of many,
not the haters, get the job done right.
I carried home the guilt of surviving
when others did not.

The Pillowcase by Midge Lorence

After Tom passed away, there was an enormous range of emotions that I felt. My body was hurting, both physically and mentally. I was so furious that he suffered for so long, and yet I was almost angry at him for leaving me behind. I didn't want to be here without him.

I started having dreams. In the most vivid one, I followed his body bag, which was an American flag, out of the hospice unit while taps were being played. His nurses lined up in the hallway as I continued to follow him out to the waiting car that would take him for cremation. This had become my nightmare on a daily basis. But it wasn't a dream because it truly happened that way.

I felt so vulnerable, lonely, and lost. How I missed him! I missed being held, and I missed feeling his breath on my neck, and a soothing hand rubbing my back telling me everything was OK and not to worry.

I slept in our king size bed and sometimes felt like the tiniest fish lost in this big sea of foam.

There was no longer anyone to reach for, or to have talks with before sleep. There was no one to kiss goodnight, wish sweet dreams and say I love you. The only things I had left, were beautiful memories and his pillow that he had taken from home and had brought into hospice. When he died, I brought it home and I treasured, and slept with it every night.

It was about six or seven months since he passed away, and I had never removed his pillowcase. I just wasn't ready to do that, not yet. In my mind, it just seemed to keep him there with me, just a bit longer. But I knew as time went on, it would be something I would have to do. And so, I began to look at that pillowcase almost as symbolic, and felt and knew in my heart, that in order to start my healing process, I would have to let go of his pillowcase. I would always have our beautiful memories and special moments tucked away in my heart forever.

One morning I arose early, and looked at the pillow I still cradled in my arms. I don't know why, but I knew today was the day. I took his pillow from our bed, hugged it tight one more time, and while tears rolled gently down my face, I delicately removed his pillowcase. It was so difficult, but I also knew it was time to try to begin my healing process.

He made me promise not to sit and wallow for months after he died. To honor his wishes, I knew It was time for me to move on to the next phase of my life which God had already planned out and I would gladly accept.

Shiva's Dance Card by Pete Ramsey

At war, in Shiva's choreography, you can be Destroyer one moment and Protector the next. Circumstances determine which you allow yourself to be on any given day.

Here, around the villages of Thanh Linh, in 1970, the back beat can be Motown or the dark despairs of Acid-rock. The stage can be as listless as the Bonneville Salt Flats or hold the intensity of Dante's 9 Circles of Hell.

We are backed up to a long jungle-covered ridge. On top is an ARVN compound and, at the foot, two distinct villes. One ville holds the families of the soldiers on top and the other those who don't share the same political viewpoint. These two groups dress in the local custom and intermingle, leaving us to guess who is who—an unenviable task for anyone, much less young men jacked on adrenaline and fear while possessing heavy weapons.

To the north rises the lower foothills of the Central Highlands with its triple canopy. In the morning, the cooler air slides down across the rice paddies and meandering stream, creating a lovely peaceful fog which washes the air clean of the smells of the various foods prepared over dried water buffalo dung fires.

To the east, past the Montagnards, the road enters a highly contested area where you might see elephant tracks in the dirt roadbed. NVA motor pool, so to speak. That route would be a pleasant ride were it not so lethal.

This morning we roll out of the valley to the west, considerably under strength and with fresh memories of losses we endured from an NVA ambush two weeks earlier on this same road.

We enter another ville, when two ducks suddenly dart across the road, and they are struck by one of our vehicles. Coincidentally a halt is called for by higher ups.

As we dismount, Mama-San runs up the road with a duck in each hand. Mama-San is clearly distraught and crying hysterically. None of us speaks Vietnamese. We attempt to compensate her with a case of

C-rations, cigarettes, and finally a big no no, Military Pay Currency. The MPC is worth more than Vietnamese piasters. She is relentless.

Unbeknownst to us is that in Vietnamese society, one's quantity of livestock determines one's level of status in the community. Our gestures cannot possibly resolve the dilemma.

The tension is reaching a seething point.

I watch the eyes and gestures of men who only two weeks earlier had witnessed six members of this unit killed at an ambush site only a couple clicks away in an all-day battle well within earshot of Mama-San. It is still raw in their memories. This ville had to have supplied both food and water for the three hundred-man NVA force which initially ambushed sixteen Americans. The villagers might have even taken care of the enemy wounded, for all we know.

We older tank commanders know it is time to go. Staying only feeds the Beast, which each man holds in check. We call our men back, mount up and pull out. We don't ask for permission from higher-ups. We just leave.

For a few moments, two totally diverse cultures stand face to face, ignorant of words and customs, each feeling grief and loss laced with frustration and anger, yet at a crucial moment, the right choice is made and we young men know it. We can live with ourselves and sleep tonight, wondering what is next on Shiva's dance card.

Tribe by Steve Henderson

My first tribe began with a youth football team in 7-8th grade. We went undefeated for two years at a little school called Woodfin, playing much larger teams. The final game in my 8th grade year was when we played against an all-star team. This to me, a 13-year-old competitor, seemed so unfair. They did not beat us, but the game was a tie. I decided to look at this score in a positive way, as the best players from other schools could not beat us…and I was so proud of that.

My second tribe was the high school Varsity football team. I was moved as a freshman to play on the varsity team for the last four games. I was so proud. My junior year we only lost one game to the number one team in the state. My senior year I was chosen as one of the two captains, which was a great honor. This year we lost about 5 games, but all were very close and we did our best.

After graduation I joined the biggest tribe of all, the USMC. Boot camp was a tough experience but a good one for me. My language and wording changed, because I was in a platoon from all across the United States. I remember stepping off the Trailways bus, and running to get on the yellow footprints. I remember the first day was to shuffle us in and cut our hair. The guy beside me did not tell the barber he had a mole on his head and the barber cut it off.

I remember getting my second wind several times … I thought I was in shape from high school athletics. But in the Marine Corp I could catch my breath and felt euphoric. I remember team week. We had mess duty at the female Marine's mess hall. I remember the first day there, the female DRI walking up and down, telling us to look at the ceiling or floor and not to be eye fucking a female recruit. I remember coming back from Elliott's Island and receiving the eagle, globe and anchor and being called a Marine for the first time!

My next tribe was in Vietnam. I remember how close we came together, knowing every secret about each other. I remember guys dying and not remembering names because the pain was too great. We all had each other's back. I remember taking the lives of the enemy and not thinking a whole lot of it.

I remember 45 years later joining another tribe...Brothers and Sisters Like These. To meet and share all of our stories and understand the times, the dangers, the emotions, has been uplifting and therapeutic for me. We have written stories and shared with our families and the public more than any of us could ever say. This tribe has become family to me.

My final tribe has been my healing group... a Moral Injury class formed for several weeks of sharing. This group has helped me to maintain stability and feel a part of what I felt with my brothers in Vietnam, although more positive and with a component of giving back to others, hoping these participants will not have to wait for 45 years to share their stories, pain and feelings.

My Scariest Moment by Tommy Cannon

My sniper team, which consisted of my spotter John and I, conducted operations on what seemed like a large island in between Fallujah and Rhamadi, Iraq. We spent a lot of time searching for enemy mortar teams and high value targets in the area. On a night mission we were moving through a wood line that was on the edge of the Euphrates River and heard a noise in the river. We took a lot of pride in the fact that we had never been spotted and although the enemy was searching us out, they never had any luck. The noise sounded a little like a boat. We froze in our positions, intently listening for other sounds. Has someone found us or heard us from the river? As a couple of splashes rang as loud as thunder and we quietly moved to a covered position. These new sounds were footsteps in the edge of the river. These footsteps were moving and getting closer. We have positioned ourselves so the only way anyone can get near us is to move in front of us. Reality was setting in, and my heart began to pound hard. In a normal gun fight, it usually happens without notice or hesitation, and as a sniper you have complete control of the fight.

Now I have time to think about our situation, and it is not good. John has an M-4 with a 203 grenade launcher, and I have a most impressive bolt action rifle. It is the best tool for its intended purpose, but not a gunfight at 10 feet. We are not wearing body armor or helmets, and preparing to engage at least a couple of men with AK-47s. So the reality is, we are in trouble. The footsteps are getting closer and my heart is pounding harder. Once they round the end of the brush, it is game on. My rifle is up and John is at the ready. At that moment we hear a strange squawking noise. It was loud, and we weren't sure what to make of it. We then saw a large crane come around the corner and make that squawking noise again. I almost yelled at that stupid bird, and I still think it might have been justified if I would have shot it.

What I Brought Back by Ted Minnick

Not sure where to begin. I've been back from Vietnam for 50 plus years, but sometimes it seems like just yesterday or even last night. I brought back some material things—a captured rifle, my jungle fatigues, my jungle boots, my K-bar knife, pictures—things I still have today. But I also brought back sensory things and perceptions. Even though I was a Commander of a Heavy Artillery Battery (I had 2-8" and 2-175s), a Quad 50-gun truck, a twin 40mm M42 Duster and should be used to loud noises, I still jump at unexpected bangs or loud noises, looking for exits or bunkers. I still don't do crowds or fireworks or screaming kids. My wife knows my triggers and suggests we leave a loud place or crowded store. I wear hearing aids today because of the artillery and we jokingly refer to my hearing loss as 'spousal deafness' or, as I like to call it, 'selective hearing'. But I can still hear a helicopter, and tell you what type, over a mile away.

I brought back an appreciation for brotherhood. My unit members (battle buddies) were my family for a year and I stay in touch with a few—we're getting smaller in number every year. I learned to depend on them to have my back and they depended on me to make sound, safe decisions. Today, I sometimes can't remember what I had for lunch or why I entered a room, but I can tell you the quadrant elevation and deflection for certain targets in our Area of Operations, or the weight of certain projectiles and powder charges; the serial number of my M14 and my M16, the names of my Battery officers and Sr NCOs. It's strange what we recall. As someone once said, "my mind can't forget what my eyes have seen."

I brought back a deeper appreciation for spouse and family. I kind of had an idea what spouse/family goes through when someone deploys—I saw it first-hand when my Dad would deploy as a pilot in the Air Force and how my Mom had to step up and do all the things that he would do if he were home plus her everyday wifely duties. I was trained to know war, how to survive its' inherent dangers and how to lead men in battle. I married my high school sweetheart from South Georgia who had no experience with military things and was suddenly thrust into a completely different lifestyle and world. When I went to Vietnam I left a wife and a 3-month-old daughter. I knew the difference between incoming and outgoing, what a tripwire sounded like, the ping of a grenade spoon, to be aware of any strange sounds—in other words to be hypervigilant to things that happen during battle. Imagine spending your days and nights dreading the sound of a car door slamming, the doorbell ringing or the telephone ringing in the middle of the night or the sight of uniformed military personnel approaching your door— imagine doing that for 365 days and nights. My wife and daughters, and other military families like them, are my heroes.

I also brought back a sneaky, hidden disease called Agent Orange Chronic Lymphocytic Leukemia—thanks to Dow Chemicals, Dioxin and Uncle Sam. I was diagnosed in 2008 (38 years after returning from Vietnam) and, thank the Good Lord, my disease remains at Stage 0—"watchful waiting," according to my oncologist. As someone once said, "not all who lost their lives in Vietnam died there and not all who came home from Vietnam ever left there." Our youngest daughter, Sarah, who was born after I returned, was diagnosed with Multiple Sclerosis in 1997 and passed away in 2016 at the age of 44. I don't hold a grudge against the Government for my disease but I feel guilty that my daughter's disease may have been caused by my exposure to Agent Orange. The VA says there is no connection but we did file a claim for her—of course, denied. As they say, "We came home and death came with us."

Lastly, I brought back a deep gratitude to the men and women of our armed services and all their sacrifices—then and now. I will always stand and salute the flag and will always thank God for those who are willing to "stand on the wall" and guard our country and what it stands for.

Untitled by Renee Hermance

I had always seen the uniform as one of pride, honor, and admiration. There is something that is carried with it that many people know and when they see the uniform, it carries instant respect.

Being a woman, the uniform carried more for me and others. W.M. Whore. Bitch. Marine. Teammate. Job title. Any moment I can fulfill any one of those titles or all of them depending on who I'm speaking with.

For me, I hadn't realized I would receive or have to carry those titles. I just wanted to do my job. However, it would not be easy. Women were rare in the military, but women marines are 1% of the military population. The whole time I was enlisted and in my field, I saw two women in my units. That is years with only one woman in each unit or not a single female in the unit. Even now, it is the proverbial unicorn when you meet another woman marine. I met a woman last summer who actually found me to connect because there are so few of us that when we meet one, we are surprised.

My time in was one of fun, great friends, comradeship, sadness, loss, murder, violence, fear, and brokenness. I had great friends. They were every race, nation, social class, and personality. We were like family. You would do anything for each other. Sometimes good or bad. Everyone had the same purpose. Even now, when I meet a fellow veteran, there is a bond immediately. We share the same humor, stories, suffering, joy, and things unique to the military. We get each other. My neighbor is from the Vietnam era. When we talk, even though we didn't serve during the same years, we can talk about the military, VA, MREs, after service challenges, and how the military has changed. A common thread.

A common thread. Every active duty member at one time or another has had to leave the military. You either retire, finish your contract, or are medically separated. Each one has its transition difficulties and reactions.

When I left the military, I thought that would be my last move. At least that was the plan. The last box went on the truck. The room was cleaned. The last few "lost" things were discovered. You know the ones.

The ones that somehow made it behind the locker or under your rack. The ones you buy a replacement for when you always had it. This is my life in two seabags, a uniform bag, my pack, and "souvenirs" from my deployments. This was all that remained.

Exhaustion, fear, and excitement all welled up in me. I was leaving my friends, the family we had become, the military family, and my life. This was going to be my old life soon, but what would be my new life? Would I speak to the people who I did life with for so many years? Would we be as close as we are after I left? What would we bond over without those Thursday night field days?

Where would I live? For years, I didn't have to worry about housing. Now, I have to think about where I would live and how would I afford it. Staying with my mom is an option. As an adult though, I would rather not. It may be the only option. This was not my plan. Now, these thoughts were a reality.

What would I do? The plan had been to make this a 20-year career then medical school. Do I go back to school? Do I take a temporary job? Can I even work or go to school? What are the realistic goals of life now? How will I make ends meet?

Again, this was not the plan. I had completed most of my requirements for MSG duty. Background checks, references, medical reviews, dental work, and a mental health check. My goals included all these things.

Now, my life looks very different. Doctor appointments, mental health checks, referrals for my doctors, and physical therapy. The social worker calling to try to find resources for better medical care, veteran socialization and actinides to help us, and how she can advocate for me. I went from abled to disabled. This is my life. Morally and medically injured. How can I go back to my "normal" life when it doesn't exist anymore? Even abnormal does not exist.

When I say that my life revolves around this, this includes night terrors, nightmares, panic attacks, flashbacks, and fear. Always fear. A prisoner now of my home and my mind. Locked in fear. A cage of loneliness surrounds me. No one is safe. Outside my wall, I'm in danger. Inside my wall, I'm safe. However, no one can come in. I can't get out. I guess this is my new "normal." Fear. Anxiety. No sleep. How do you live to your fullest when your body and mind are not on board? So much for going home as I was.

My therapist says radical acceptance. Radical acceptance of what I saw, what happened to me, and what happened to my teammates. I struggle with this. The moral injury. How do we make peace with murder, loss, fear, and numbness? Is it better to continue to be numb all the time? Is this a good thing that I live with and in? No fear. No love. No worry. No joy. No anger. No openness. No feelings. Numb. Are no feelings better than the ones that I avoid? Am I really living? No, but no protects everyone and me. Is this the way with radical acceptance to feel everything we closed off to survive? Now I need to feel, but don't want to deal with the fallout of those emotions. I need to cry. I need to be angry. To scream.

With all of those emotions comes a messiness I don't want to face. The yelling. The hurting others. The breaking crap. The fear. The depression. The suicidal thoughts. The survivors' guilt. The hurting myself. The whys.

The "why did I live and they didn't?" I don't feel like I should have been the one at times. What if I had died, would it have prevented the second death? Where's the justice? Do I really want justice? How do I make peace with all of this? Do I give up the part of me which hasn't resolved this and what will take the place of that? Radical acceptance of that girl before everything exploded and fell apart? Can I ever be that girl before the loss of that day? Can we ever get to the part of radical acceptance in our lives which says that sucked and evil exists but I can live life?

One day I hope I will be able to have radical acceptance. I believe I will be able to accept this part of my life. One day I'll be able to lie my head down to sleep without the nightmares. I'll be able to have close relationships with others without expecting the worse. Radical acceptance will be achievable even if right now I can't see it or believe it.

Arrival by Michael White

It wasn't the 16 hour, 524 or so all grunt, cramped passenger flight from Anchorage, AK to Kuwait.

It wasn't the month-long wait on an oceanless beach that reminded us all of what may have been the most relaxing field exercise ever.

It wasn't during that time that rumors began to stir of sniper threats beyond what seemed like a lonely land, a place that looked like a Martian planet.

Oh, it definitely wasn't the veering out of a small circular window of a hotdog shaped helicopter, that to our surprise turned out to be one of the most exhilarating roller coaster rides that shot fireworks from the side of the strangest looking cities, of mud and stone rooftops with buildings built like a child-spilt Lego box.

And it wouldn't be the other soldiers that ran to and fro, all in gear, weapons slung, getting in and out of humvees, frantically packing ammo, cans of water, and other gear, as they slowly moved out like an accordion, single file, kicking up dust as we watched and tiredly stood in formation awaiting to be shown where we would sleep, as we tried to make out what the platoon Sergeant was saying, sounding like some actor from a black and white silent film.

It was definitely that night though, not even having unpacked, sometime in the late, late night when all should have been silent, only instead, feeling the bed and the air around me vibrate so violently as if it were taking my breath, and simultaneously my roommate springing into action and frantically ushering me to hurry while a siren blares outside as I rush out the door into chaos.

More Than a Drop by John Sitman

I spent all my time up on the DMZ.
I flew in a Medevac Huey where most walked
and humped thru jungle and trees.
Flying out of Quang Tri responding to a call,
we saddled up and headed out in late fall.
The coordinates brought us to a jungle floor.
An ambush had taken place the night before.
We picked up wounded and brought them through the doors.
Some of the soldier's receiving life-threatening needs
that demanded our immediate attention in stopping them bleed.
I went through the motions of helping these men
just as I've done for others before them.
Holding plasma, giving comfort, saying, "we would be there soon,"
or "try and hold on," was the common message from us few.
We finally get them to the triage where we flew down to get them in.
Later, as I clean off the deck seeing from the days flight,
I begin to recall the echo of the days fight.
It became another day I wore on my hands and clothes
the blood of my brothers whose names were unknown.
Their blood stains covered me like splattered paint,
spilling so indiscriminately all over the place.
I felt the burden and weight of their life changing fate
that weighed heavy and deep and becoming so great.
I would have preferred the color of clay or mud
or the stench of fatigues worn and torn from the jungle and sun.
Instead, I wore their blood with anguish and fresh pain,
recognizing their need from receiving deep wounds that day.
There was no distinction between any blood type;
it could have been "A" or "B,"

or from O positive to O negative type.

It didn't matter, it was all red,

flowing from each one of them.

It was a premium liquid, like a rare gem,

this red fluid that was coming from within them.

I wore this color and its odor like it was part of my uniform,

like a unit patch, insignia, or rank that was worn,

because it was part of the routine of everyday war

When it was exposed, it began taking on different forms,

turning things rotten with a stench down to the core.

When it flowed, it changed whatever it touched from clothing, to

bandages, to the body it left.

I spent time trying to wash it off.

Scrubbing and scrubbing and not able to tell

if I had gotten it all off or not,

turning my skin raw and red

because it clung to me like part of my skin.

It became morbid when worn all day, drying hard as a shell.

It kept you aware of its presence and soldiers as it continued to smell.

It came with the uncertainty of recovery to its blame.

Its flow carried with it sorrow and unimaginable pain.

It only stopped when the right pressure, tourniquet,

or dressing was maintained,

or when it ran out and completely drained.

The deeper the wound, the louder the screams,

only to stop from the shock it would bring.

This was not from strange or distant men;

this was from our own soldiers, trying to defend.

The burden was heavy, even without knowing names

from an element of mental and physical strain.

Its infection can continue to press

as I wake in a cold and unfiltered sweat,

when one of them comes to me in a nightmare exposing again the whole days event.

It is the common color and fluid of war.

I cry out, "Please, no more!"

Untitled by Kevin Weirman

PROLOGUE

For those of us that may have on an occasion or three or four, colored slightly outside the lines, adjusting to military life is tough. Adapting to civilian life after our military experience can be tougher. I was invited to speak to graduates and current participants of the N.C. Veterans Treatment Court program at their annual Christmas Party. These are military men and women who, like me, had made a mistake or two but were granted an opportunity to 'make it right' while putting them in a position to steer their lives in a positive direction. This is what I said to them.

VETERANS COURT CHRISTMAS PARTY - DEC 2021

Gimme a minute here. I am afraid to start before the ink is completely dry. I do not want to admit that I wait to the last minute to get stuff done, but truth be told, I just really do not like doing this. I get all worked up and all emotional. Yeah, I will get choked up several times and probably cry, at least once. I shake and stutter and sweat and it is really not a whole lot of fun. So, I had to ask myself, "Why the hell did I agree to put myself through this, again?" It boiled down to this, I am very selfish. I realize that doing this is good for me and helps me on my journey. So yeah, me first. Then I thought about the possibility that even if only one sentence that I manage to stumble through can help even just one of you on your path, that would make me feel so awesome! So, it really is all about me.

I must confess though, when Steve told me that you were the people that I would be attempting to read for, I was actually excited. Believe it or not, I too, have experienced being on the unfavorable side of the law myself. I know what you are thinking, no, no way, not this clean cut, handsome, sharp dressed, self-confident, and articulate guy. But yeah, it really did happen. Thankfully only once and quite some time ago. But I will get into that at some point, I hope.

First, I have to tell you yet another reason why I do not like doing this. I have this tremendous fear of being misunderstood...of being judged. Whenever I start writing something that I will read to others, I always feel like I have to tell you my whole life story so that you will know and understand everything about me. That way, you might like me or at least accept me as I am. I learned the hard way, as have you, that in the real world, that simply does not happen very often. However, Thank God, you and I have found some truly good people and places where it is true most of the time. Never expect perfection in any person or any institution devised by people, or we will be disappointed every time. Except in the case of the person whose Holiday we are celebrating. He will never fail you and if you want to hear more about Him, I will be happy to speak with you at length another time.

Remember, this is about me.

Back to my life story and I am only 57 and have been everywhere and done everything so this should not take too long, but you may want to get comfortable. To start I was born on Friday the 13th. You can probably fill in the rest yourselves... and please feel free to use your imagination. OK.

Military:	Navy Nuclear Propulsion Submariner 1981-1990
	Navy Reserve SEABEE 2001-2008 – (Iraq 2005)
	Navy Reserve In Shore Boat Unit – (United Arab Emirates 2006)
	Medically Retired May 2008

The reason I was looking forward to speaking to you is because I think that I sort of, kind of, have a bit more in common with you than our Military experience. When I first got back to Hendersonville in 2007, well, I was mess. It is all still really hazy so here is the general scoop. I was on over 20 VA provided medications and just really struggling physically, mentally & emotionally. I drank a bellyful of miscellaneous alcohol and ate a bunch of pills and drove to get more beer. The clerk called the cops, and all hell broke loose. I ended up locked up and transferred to VA Psych Ward.

I had a laundry list of charges: Assaulting an Officer X3 (in my defense, they all tased me first) Resisting Arrest, Public Drunkenness, Disorderly Conduct, Trespassing, Disturbing the Peace, DUI & more, I am sure. I had heard something about a Veterans Court System being set up and cannot remember if it was available yet or not and did not know anything about it. I do remember that my Public Defender and the DA had a soft spot for troubled Vets, and they spoke to the Officers & Judge, and they all came up with a plan to make it as painless as possible. It did help that I had very good rapport with all Hendersonville Police before leaving for Iraq. So, they agreed to drop all charges except the DUI, but no jail, and I do not remember how much the fines were, if any.

Moral of the story: Take advantage of resources available and breaks given, if any. There are very good people out there willing to work with us and for us if we are at least willing to put in the effort to grow and work toward improving ourselves.

EPILOGUE

As of this writing, I am aware of one in attendance that evening that has joined the Brothers & Sisters Like These writing group to further advance his healing. So yes, my shaking, stuttering, sweating, anxiety and all the rest was worth every second it took to get those words out. Today there are so many very different ways that we Wounded Warriors can receive guidance getting onto a path of healing that may lead us to a greater sense of purpose, self-acceptance, forgiveness, and inner peace. I encourage you, no I beg you, to try as many as it takes to find the one(s) that fit your needs. Have not we lost too many Brothers & Sisters already? I pray that God will be with you on your journey. BE SAFE!

Tags by James Watts

In 1971 I placed my military belongings away, but they were far from being forgotten.

In the darkest corner of my closet is a box that measures 2 x 2 x 2. Inside the box are items of my military life untouched in a lot of years, by choice. I picture this young man of only eighteen years of age and willing but unknowing of things to come. In the end, things you would never want to tell.

In this box I slowly open, I have personal and private items, a camouflage helmet cover with "South Carolina" in bold print, M60 machine gun rounds, five or six showing their age, dress khakis neatly folded, dress shoes that really need a polish, number letters and correspondence from the world back home with imaginary plans and promises of the things we would do if I made it back to the US in one piece. Deeper in the box were other items from the era of the Vietnam War such as rank insignia, olive drab caps and finally my jungle boots, black with green webbing for ventilation. The boots are worn but still bear a dog tag threaded through the left boot lace, and close by was a chain with the other dog tag. The tags were military issued and although they were small in size they gave me a great feeling of pride because of the information they possessed. Last name, initials, service number, branch of service, religion and blood type.

This is me. My life may mean nothing to others but means everything to me. After every mission I would take time to identify the young soldier who wore these dog tags so special to the North and South portions of my body. I think somehow they helped me to keep focused. Just do your job, don't overthink, keep alert, say your prayers daily and hopefully return home, a place you never thought was so important until you couldn't get there.

Although the time has gone by, the memories rush through my mind and quickly I choose not to remember the box in the darkest corner of my walk-in closet.

A Promise is a Promise by Donna Culp

The Navy recruiter at our high school said to go to nursing school and after graduation to come see him and he would be honored to sign me up. My Dad made me promise that if I went into the military to do so as an officer.

One semester after I started nursing school at Texas Women's University, I found my passion in Occupational Therapy (OT). After graduation, passing my boards, and in the process of interviewing for jobs I was sitting at a traffic light in Arlington, Texas, and had one of those "Ah-Ha!" moments. Looking to my right there it was. The military recruiting office for all the branches of the military.

Pulling into the parking lot, saying a quick prayer for God's guidance, I parked my car, and walked into the office. After introducing myself, it was quick business. The Navy and the Marines didn't have OT billets. The Army didn't have any at the time and none on the horizon. The Air Force didn't have any billets at the time but knew there would be some billets coming up. He put a huge star on my file and promised to stay in touch.

Over the next five years I worked in the civilian sector, figuring out my areas of special interest. It was during this time that I helped establish licensure for OTs in Texas, established two OT clinics in two different hospitals, and met an Active Duty USAF LtCol OT at a hand rehabilitation conference in Philadelphia.

After talking with her I felt more comfortable with the idea of changing my civilian life to military life.

Then one day the recruiter called and said the OT billet was opening and we needed to start the process of getting me cleared for raising my hand. With that I sought final council with my boss, Wayne, for validation. Always pragmatic, honest, and an overall great boss, he weighed in on my decision. Reminding me that the hospital had hit a financial bump in the road resulting in a hiring freeze, no upward mobility for anyone for the foreseeable future, he encouraged me to go raise my hand. He then told me that if at any time I decided the military wasn't going to be a twenty-year career, I could always return to Huguley Hospital and have my job back. A win-win either way.

After rescheduling my last two patients, I left work and headed straight to the recruiter's office, raised my hand, and made a promise I honor to protect and defend the Constitution of the United States against enemies, foreign and domestic.

Since that day I have repeated that oath several times, and every time it takes me back to that afternoon in Arlington, Texas. Although no longer in the military, and now retired from the Federal Government, I maintain that this vow remains unbroken. A promise is a promise.

Here Was a Man by Daniel Anest

I guess I'll start this by saying that I've never really had a desire to tell violent "war stories" or rehash losses that I have had to deal with. But going back to a time I don't often enjoy reflecting on, there are some… well one event, that without any doubt in my mind, set the tone for my career and my intentions when it came to doing my job. It was one of the first nights that my section was tasked with overwatching an MSR (main supply route) that was often used to transport HVTs (high valued targets) as well as be a very popular stretch of road to place IEDs for the enemy. I, like I'm sure most Americans that had witnessed 9/11 and enlisted to get some payback, had my eye buried in my ACOG (scope on a weapon), anxious to drop the hammer on anyone that gave me just about any reason.

I was lying about fifty meters out to the right flank of my truck in the designated marksmanship position doing my best to stay concentrated on my sector of fire while dealing with the never-ending moon dust making its way down the front of my skivvy shirt. When I heard my section leader's voice come on my personal radio to mount up. As fast as I could, I broke my position and sprinted to my truck in hopes we were en route to a fight. I loaded up in the Humvee slamming myself up against the tow missiles that took up almost half of the head room for me to sit comfortably behind the driver. The section leader came over the comm that we were "Oscar Mike" to a thermal signature that one of the tow gunners had picked up some kilometers away from our overwatch position. I can't be a hundred percent sure what was going through my head, but I can be fairly confident that my hand was shaking uncontrollably as my thumb flipped the selector switch on my M-4 from safety to semi as fast as it could.

Very luckily for me and my possible enemies in the future, fate had other plans for me than having to use my trigger finger that night. As we approached the thermal signature it became clear that it was nothing more than a shepherd with his flock of sheep. I can be fairly certain that even as the interpreter was explaining to my section leader that the man had NO IDEA why Americans were in Iraq, he offered tea and pita bread to us. I was still suspicious of his nefarious plans for us. It really wasn't until some weeks later of observing the life and death struggles and decisions that people living in the desert had to make daily, and some time to reflect within myself, that I could really appreciate what that shepherd had done.

Here was a man that didn't hate my way of life, didn't care about what religion I practiced and certainly didn't have any intentions of causing myself or any of my Marines any harm. Here was a man that had nothing more than the tent he graciously invited us into, the two mules that carried his tent and other equipment, and his flock of sheep. Yet he chose to deplete his own provisions that were vital to his and his flock's survival for complete strangers. Strangers that rolled up on him with big loud trucks that I am sure disturbed his flock, aiming weapons at him with the worst prejudiced attitudes and intentions for him.

I know for a fact that even now, almost two decades later, if I were placed in that position I would do my best, if not with a weapon or with anything else at my disposal, to communicate with these foreign assholes that had just woken me up and scared the hell out of my animals, how unhappy I was with their actions and their presence in my country.

But here was a man who was wise enough to not let his emotions dictate his behaviors. Kind enough to share what he needed to survive, and gracious enough to invite us into his home.

Here was a man that taught me a valuable lesson that I'm still learning from to this day.

Here was a man that needed my protection from the real enemy.

Here was a man that showed us such an immense amount of character, that risking my life to protect his way of life was acceptable.

Here was a man, not a target, and not my enemy.

The Things They Carried by Dorian Dula

What I carried in Vietnam was pretty basic. An extra pair of socks, maybe an extra pair of underwear, several weeks' worth of C Rations in my pack with Sterno, Tabasco Sauce, several loaded M-16 magazines, two canteens, a pocket-sized prayerbook, hydroxychloroquine tablets and my flak jacket. Sometimes we carried bandoleers of M-60 Machine Gun ammo for the Machine Gunners. No photos that I carried. I had a photo of my younger brother and sister back with my gear in the rear.

For a while a picture of my girlfriend when we went to the Prom, but she didn't wait and couldn't even make it through the 11 weeks I was gone in Bootcamp. She was with someone else by the time I got home from Bootcamp. So, I tore it up and threw it away. But I carried that pain of betrayal. Every woman I ever loved betrayed me and left me for someone else, except my wife, who I married when I was 37. But those betrayals are a story for another time.

The physical things I carried were what was needed to stay alive in the bush as we called it. I read this excerpt from this gentleman's book, The Things They Carried, about his getting hot chow and ice cold beer every few weeks. What a bunch of crap that was. Not my unit. We got hot chow maybe twice in my whole tour and beer maybe once a month, so hot you could barely drink it. Apparently, the author wasn't a Marine.

In-country, I started mentally carrying visions of my friends getting killed and seeing their lifeless bodies. A guy I had bunker watch with the night before, who talked about his family and when he played high school football and caught the game-winning touchdown in an Idaho State playoff game. Now he is the lifeless body of a nineteen-year-old kid who died for his country.

Unfortunately, there were many more visions of eighteen, nineteen, and twenty-year-olds I knew that died. Visions of going to Graves Registration, which was basically a field morgue and you had to identify your friends who died. And I then said, Yes, that's Toyer, Cox, Chavous, Sawaya and so many others. Yeah, I carried that as a nineteen-year-old and I still carry that as a seventy-four-year-old.

I carry the day I was shot, February 18th, 1968. I was the Squad Leader who had a Machine Gun Team with us. I was in charge of 13 men. It hit the fan that morning and Boice, Warren and Berry died and all the rest of us were wounded. I survived. Why?? I was wounded but had to keep my wits about me and keep us under control on the Radio with our command. We were pinned down for an hour. Eventually other Marines came and got us out. When they took us back to the Battalion Aid Station (BAS) and they loaded me off the stretcher to take me in, there was a sight I will carry until I'm buried at Arlington. Outside of the BAS were dead Marines in body bags, stacked up like a cord of wood.

They took care of the most seriously wounded first of course, and I saw Sammy, a black kid from Louisiana, and he had bandages over his eyes and he heard my voice and he yelled, "Dula." They brought him over and we hugged and cried. I never saw him again. I hope he didn't lose his sight. Yes, I carry that day, February 18th, 1968 to this day.

I carry the day I was in the Hospital in Cam Rahn Bay and the Doctor came in and told me I was going to a Hospital in Japan to recover. I told him I was in Japan for R&R and he said, "really, how long have you been in country?" and I told him almost 11 months. And he said, "Marine, you are going home." And I started crying.

The flight home was 16 hours, but was the best flight of my life.

I carry leaving the Hospital in Oakland, CA, where I was for six weeks, on a shuttle bus taking us to the train station, airport, or Bus Station, so we could go home and the Anti-War protesters outside the gate with nasty derogatory signs, and they were throwing bottles and rocks at us and chanting "Murderers." Many on the bus were amputees. I carry going to class a few years later at San Jose St. University where I would later get my degree, going to class one morning and there was some protest rally going on and there were some assholes on the stage giving speeches and an enemy flag of the North Vietnamese Army (NVA).

I was so upset I couldn't go to class and went back to my house and never went to that class.

Those are just some of the things I carry.

Montagnard Bliss by Bruce Turek

"Montagnard" is the French word for "people of the mountains"
civil affairs had one more seat on the slick that day.
they were headed to a Montagnard village
farther up in the central highland mountains, north of pleiku.
their purpose was to promote good will.
our patrol took on the look
not of combat troops,
but of a cabin-full of newspaper hacks.
we did, though, have weapons, flak jackets and steel pots.
.........oh. and a tape recorder.

after flying probably 45 minutes,
our pilot set the chopper down
so we could jump off
and set out to see the village.
we somehow found it, hidden from view in the air
by tall pine trees and underbrush.
approaching, we could see
that the villagers knew we were coming.

lined up on either side of the path
were ALL the natives;
mama-san, topless, children hiding behind their mothers,
the men in sarongs and the chief, framed behind all of them.
he came forward to welcome us through our interpreter,
smiling broadly, gesturing for us to
continue and follow him into the village
to a focal point, a bare, well-used and packed dirt meeting place.

we westerners sat with all the others circling the fire.
the chief, his subjects and their kids
squatted comfortably, just like down in the delta,
where unconcerned farmers hunkered down, defecating.

I unwittingly, maybe, had chosen a spot
almost touching a huge, three by three-foot earthen pot
filled to the brim with a dark liquid
with a salad of leaves and herbs innocently floating on its top.

their leader, Jarai, honored us, smiling.
then, without hesitation, passed around a gourd
and pointed out that their wine was unsurpassed.
it was sitting there, in the urn, under the foliole.

2

he then made it known that all of us
were expected to participate, to celebrate our visit,
by drinking out of the gourd,
after dipping it into, but under, the salad.

demonstrating the art, he dunked the vessel
down into the brew, brought it to his lips
and drank generously.
since I was closest, he handed me the cup.
following his lead, I submerged it,
got me a heaping measure, closed my eyes,
prayed to the wine gods about sanitation,
then drew a long, cool, sip of their concoction.
passing the cup to the next celebrant,
I suddenly realized that this stuff was potent.
I therefore couldn't wait until it was again my turn.

we all happily partook, the villagers and us,
men, women but no children.
I gained new admiration
for their code for familial propriety.
as the afternoon weighed on, the sillier we got.
then our army leader, captain griffin,

stood, reached into his pouch
and pulled out the tape recorder.

apparently, he had done this before.
he turned it on, recorded a few words,
stopped, backed up the tape
and played back the sound of his voice.
you'd have thought lightning had struck.
from the chief down to the smallest child,
to a person, they were silent and awestruck.
the recorder was new to them. then the fun began.

the captain managed to convey to the chief
that he should say a few words into the recorder.
he did. the tape was rewound, then played back.
lightning struck again.

try to imagine the word dumbstruck.
the excitement they all felt hearing his recorded voice was flabbergast-
edly tangible.
laughter, joy, applause and wild exuberance by all
who careened around the campfire; it was a joyous moment.

and that, dear friends, was Montagnard bliss.

There Can Be No Land of the Free Without the Home of the Brave
by Anne Adkins

Today I want to tell you about 9/11 and the effect it had on our family and son, who was killed on May the 3rd of 2007 in Iraq. But first a little more about Matthew.

When he was little, he asked us for his first toys. He wanted toy soldiers, then toy tanks, then more military games. His favorite channel? The History Channel of course. He said the best war was World War II. When I asked why, his little voice said, "Mama, don't you know bad people hurt us, but we fought them and that was what saved our country?" I drew down and hugged him, burying my nose is his neck, looking so forward to the unique smell he was born with—originally, conviction and the incredible sweetness of wildflower honey.

We were a good family with a good life, but our family changed on the terrible day of 9/11. Like everyone, we were devastated at what had happened to our country that terrible day, but Matthew was more than that. He transformed from disbelief to devastation, then to anger and finally, commitment. He sat us down and said he was going to enlist in the Army. He had considered it for days and realized that it was what he was supposed to do. His intent was that something like this would never happen to our country again. Never again. Ever.

We received many letters and phone calls from him during his first tour. During our calls I would ask him questions about his service and he always said, "it's ok." But there was such strain in his voice, I imagined I saw dirt flying off the ground after enemy fire and body bags in the distance. He always evaded answering me. He never wanted me to worry. I could tell that, so I stopped inquiring.

Immediately following his homecoming from his first tour the first thing he did was ask if we could go to New York. When we landed, Ground Zero was the first place he wanted to go. We arrived and he just stood looking at the devastation for so long. So long. Then suddenly he turned to me and I saw a single tear roll down his beautiful cheek and he gathered me in his arms in a fierce hug. I buried myself in his neck again and smelled him—conviction and the incredible sweetness of wildflower honey. He drew back and looked at me and I saw his love for me in his eyes. He then said, "Mama there are some things worth dying for, and that is my family and my country."

After only one month home following his first tour, he called us and said he was going back to Iraq early. "Why oh why, you don't have to yet," we said and he explained to us that if he went back early troops with families could stay home with their families longer. He said it was the right thing to do and that someday someone would do the same for him.

Then came the day no parent wants to live through. Our son had been killed. Pain like I had never felt hit me like a bullet. I could not stand it. I wanted to die. The pain was in every part of my mind and body. It was so bad I went numb. Numbness was the only way I could deal with the pain and then after a couple of months, God help me. I thawed. How could we live without him? I thought so hard about killing myself but could not do that to my daughter and husband. But I was not alone in my pain. Matthew's sister Emma was also totally lost in her own grief and pain.

Unbeknownst to us, after Matthew's death she started taking prescription drugs to help her pain, and the drugs got stronger and stronger, ending up with her a heroin addict. The most frightening thought I have ever had was the possibility of losing both my children, but then reality rose. She needed help and we got it for her. She has now finally accepted that while Matthew is physically gone, he still remains deeply within her. She has been clean for four years.

Then several months after Matthew's death I received a call from two of his best Army friends. They sounded so sad when they called and finally they said, "Mama, we have to tell you something. It's really hard but Matthew made us promise." They said they were with Matthew when he died and he looked up at them and said, "It's ok guys. Really. But I am really worried about my mother so please call her and tell my mama it's ok. Tell her to remember what I said at ground zero. Tell her

I am not afraid." He then grabbed their hands, drew his last breath and went to a better place.

Nine\Eleven represents our son's dedication to his country—which ultimately led to his tragic death! But he was where he wanted to be, doing what he was determined to do. Think about that and think how lucky this country is to have had young men and women who enlisted to defend against that dreadful attack. And I also am doing what I was determined to do after his death. I quit my job and began my commitment to make sure those who died for their country are remembered and those who need help get the help they so need. Please remember all of them and their heroism and the families that have sadly been left behind. But most importantly, always remember this. We can never be the land of the free without being the home of the brave.

Mt. Tamalpais Revisited—Coming Home from Vietnam
by Allan Perkal

Fifty-plus years ago I faced a crossroad in my life—this is my story.

It was 1973, five years after returning from Vietnam. I was crashing in my old Opel Kadett on top of Mt. Tamalpais, in Northern California. My life was at a crossroads. I was homeless and severely depressed, with no sense of meaning and purpose.

I had no mission—many years removed from my tour in Vietnam—where I took care of the wounded. I didn't seem to fit in, I was a different person than the one who went to Vietnam. I was isolated and feeling alone.

Waking up one foggy morning in the back seat, hungry and cold, a lightning bolt hit.

Stop feeling sorry for yourself—have you forgotten who you are? You owe it to yourself and those who never returned and those who returned differently to live your life to its fullest—with renewed meaning and purpose.

My dedication to the mission of taking care of the wounded, physically and psychologically, has sustained me ever since.

I will always remember and never forget what I carried forth from that mountain peak. It was the beginning of my healing journey coming home from Vietnam.

Memories of Vietnam, 67-68, that I carry in my medic bag are there as a constant reminder of that special time and place. I would like to tell you about a significant one dedicated to the caretakers who witnessed the cost of war.

Hospitals are a place of tears, where one is opened up to all our fears. A place where one goes within to find out the meaning of your ills. When you wake up and find out life is not a dream, that your mirror has been broken and all can be seen. You say to yourself, life goes on within you and without you. So, your position is clearly seen, are you still back in the Nam or have you come home on that freedom bird having healed those wounds of war?

Where would I be if it wasn't for Brothers And Sisters Like These?

Together then, together again!

From "FNG" to Full-Fledged Warrior: Vietnam to Desert Storm
by Alton Whitley

By the time I arrived in Vietnam in 1970, it was apparent our country was waning in its commitment to an unpopular war. I was just a "young buck" 1st Lieutenant (LT), commonly referred to as an FNG. What I really wanted to do was to become a full-fledged combat fighter pilot in the F-100. Until I achieved that goal, I would remain an FNG under the watchful eyes of the older, seasoned aviators of my unit, the 531st Tactical Fighter Squadron (TFS) "Ramrods." This was a tight knit group of fighter pilots. They loved to have fun with the new LTs. They seldom passed up on the opportunity to challenge and teach the ropes to the five of us who had arrived together to finally rid ourselves of the much-dreaded label.

These seasoned aviators did not want us to become a statistic. Not because they had taken a liking to us or because we had become close to them. They simply didn't want to go through the trouble of gathering, packing, and sending our stuff to a grieving wife, children or parents of a fighter pilot lost. They knew snotty nosed LTs could be naïve, cocky and semi-dangerous. It was easier on them if they just kept us alive by teaching us the ropes than it was to take care of the duties and requirements because of our demise.

One of the last milestones we had to accomplish to become combat ready was to complete our checkout on the night alert pad. Night flying was already inherently dangerous. Your depth perception, bad weather, cockpit lighting and vertigo can all play tricks on your mind, especially at night. The F-100 cockpit lighting for night flying was lousy. The panels, gauges and instruments often had inconsistent levels of illumination. Some of the armament switches were hard to see and manage in the heat of battle, especially at night. Individually, none of these were a big deal. Dealing with all these issues at night in a dynamic situation could easily lead to disorientation or confusion that could prove deadly. None of that really seemed to matter at the time for I thought I was an invincible fighter pilot and I thought there was nothing I couldn't do. I did not feel so invincible 20 years later when I flew America's first stealth fighter over Baghdad the first night of Desert Storm. Time, aging, experience, the loss of fellow aviators, marriage and fatherhood will do that to you.

I will never forget that first night sortie off the alert pad at Bien Hoa Airbase when the klaxon sounded. Our headquarters was scrambling two F-100s from the 531st TFS to help a unit in a bind in III Corps. At the blast of the klaxon, everyone hustled about the alert pad taking care of their assigned duties. Frankly, it startled me at first. I hesitated momentarily but quickly got it together, gathered a few items and out the door I went. After a quick glance at my aircraft, I was up the ladder of my single seat jet and crawled into the cockpit. The crew chief followed me up the ladder and made sure I was buckled into my parachute and strapped into the ejection seat. We started engines, checked in on the radio, requested taxi instructions and headed to the last chance area. That's where a small maintenance and armament crew gave us a final check of our aircraft and ordnance before we pulled onto the runway. In the cockpit I only had to remember one pin before we rolled down the runway - my ejection seat pin. Overlooking that little pin could cost your life if you failed to remove it.

After we were cleared for takeoff, we ran our engines up to full military power. My leader released his brakes and lit the afterburner of his Pratt and Whitney J-57 engine. A long orange plume of fire stretched far out of the back of his airplane dancing off the runway surface. I followed him 15 – 20 seconds later. There's no doubt our noisy departure awakened many who were trying to get some sleep, but it meant help was on the way for some friendly troops in distress. The weather was good, so I had no problem tracking my leader's lights for the join-up as we headed south to the target area. The mission took us somewhere in the southern part of III Corps and things went pretty much as planned. We put our ordnance where the Forward Air Controller directed us. While not a factor on this night, things could get a little hairy when the friendlies were screaming at the FAC for help, yet it was almost impossible to distinguish definitive lines between the good guys and the bad guys, especially at night.

Halfway through my tour I moved to Tuy Hoa Airbase along the coast in II Corps and was assigned to the 309th TFS "Wild Ducks." Our night missions at Tuy Hoa were of a different nature because of the rising mountainous terrain to the north and west of our location.

There was no "Welcome Home" in late 1970 when I came home. I came home to a broken marriage and learned it was only another dimension of the phrase "War is Hell."

I returned to the Vietnam war in early 1973, flying the much more sophisticated A-7D Corsair assigned to the 3rd TFS, a search and rescue unit stationed in Thailand. This was just after Operation Linebacker II in December 1972 that brought the North Vietnamese to their senses. As the war wound down, we flew primarily close air support as well river and road convoy escort missions in Cambodia. Many of us returning for a tour in the A-7D were seasoned combat pilots who had completed a tour in the F-100 or F-105. We had several young LTs in that unit; they had "earned their spurs" during Operation Linebacker II despite their limited experience.

In 1970 I could never have imagined that some 20 years later, I would be flying America's first stealth fighter, the F-117, and commanding another generation of FNGs when they found themselves in the skies of Iraq on the first night of Desert Storm. As we dropped our laser guided bombs in the stunning barrage of anti-aircraft artillery and surface to air missiles we encountered, I once again felt that same rush of adrenaline I had experienced on that first night mission off the alert pad in Vietnam flying the F-100. Despite my age and experience in Desert Storm, I'll be the first to admit the 19 missions in that war were both scary and exhilarating. In some ways I still felt like an FNG trying to earn my own spurs. I was also old and seasoned enough to know I was not invincible by any means.

Fortunately, American ingenuity and stealth technology allowed us to make precision strikes throughout Iraq with a sophisticated weapons delivery system that allowed us to find our intended target at night and use a laser to guide our bombs to our assigned targets despite horrific enemy air defenses. Most of the guys flying the F-117 in Desert Storm had never been to war. However, they certainly received a baptism by fire. They quickly became full-fledged warriors as they achieved unprecedented success in aerial warfare. In Desert Storm, our success in taking out our assigned strategic targets accelerated the defeat of a once formidable Iraq military and ultimately saved the lives of many on the ground. It demonstrated the value of stealth technology that was later incorporated into the design of weapons systems like the B-2, F-22 and F-35. Amazingly, we eventually brought all our people and all of our aircraft home.

I belong to a Healing Group of veterans, the majority of which are Army or Marine veterans of Vietnam. I realize one of them could have easily been on the ground that night in the spring of 1970 when I flew that first night mission off the alert pad. None of us were heroes. All of us were warriors doing our duty, yet each of us was an FNG at some point. All gave something in combat. Some gave everything. Many of us are watching fellow veterans "Flying West" as we say in the Air Force, as Father Time takes his toll. All of us left our youthful innocence and part of our heart and soul in the ungodly and unforgiving places we served whether it be Vietnam, Iraq, or Afghanistan. Another group of warriors known as "Brothers and Sisters Like These" has helped many of us put to rest events and memories that kept us off balance for a long time after we saw combat. Not only are we blessed to have found one another, but also to be led and proctored by professionals who are genuinely interested in helping veterans and their families to deal with the impact of their loved one's combat experiences.

Loss or Lost by Michael White

For a period of my life around these mountains and hills of concrete like paper in the wind. A rain puddle often mirrored a faithless drifter with a broken heart. For a time, I would unsuccessfully fill the void in my chest with delusions of half measures when all I needed to do is surrender.

The Banana Cat by Pete Ramsey

It is a fairly quiet morning here in Thanh-Linh. The fog has cleared and the village is stirring about. The only reason I am here is because I had just been assigned to a Sheridan tank. They had been designed for battle on the plains of Eastern Europe and were thus technologically advanced. All weapons systems were electrically operated and subject to shorting out. The manufacturer had specifically warned against deployment to humid climates. Thus it was the first place the Army sent them. They broke down a lot which gave some of us a break from combat operations. It would have been more pleasant to me however if we were not totally immobile, practically no perimeter, and surrounded by stacks of artillery rounds in boxes as high as the tank itself. An open ground ammo dump. One mortar round or satchel charge and, well.

Soon the kids will show up in the hope of making money off of the Americans coming and going near the runway. Normally they want us to buy Vietnamese beer or rum or do errands for us, but the opportunities are slim.

One kid seems to be excited about what he has to offer and even though I am wary to let him near me with any suspicious object in hand, I do so anyway. He then surprises me with this little dark creature with a long hairy tail and enormous eyes for his overall size, which is maybe a foot long total. He is not skittish at all and obviously nocturnal. He crawls right onto my hand and up around my neck and shoulders he goes. His paws are like moistened spongy pads, cool in touch. The kid says he is a banana cat and would I like to buy him.

Now you might be wondering why I am even entertaining such a thought as having a pet given the circumstances of the realities I exist in. But I guess that is just the point. The total absurdity of the life of a combat soldier is not lost on us. Every day we are faced with the utter frailty of life and the gossamer thread we hold on to it by is more akin to a spider's web than a ship's Hauser. Absurdity becomes a drinking partner.

The little guy holds an appeal. He is not aggressive. He exudes calmness and tranquility. He is just what I need in a search for normalcy in an insane environment. He allows himself to be stroked and handled. Already the frayed and raw nerves of my life are seeking relief. A sense of kindness and caring are taking hold in me. Wow, they still exist. Whatever difficulties keeping him might present will be dealt with. Predictions are speculative at best.

Later this evening and on successive evenings he climbs the whip antenna on the tank and pulls guard duty with me, never offering to leave, then returns to my pocket. He is at peace in there and for a time my soul snuggles right there with him, oblivious to its tattered state.

Flak Jacket by Ron Toler

The thing we wore to keep us safe,

to protect the vital parts from incoming.

To protect our bodies from the rockets placed on Charlie Ridge and pointed toward the base.

The thing we thought we left behind on the long flight back to the "world."

But had we left it behind?

Hadn't we really replaced it with an invisible shield of full body armor?

Body armor that protected us from the slings and arrows of our fellow man.

Body armor that held in the loss of youth, the anger, at times the rage, the sorrow

for what we had seen and done.

We couldn't share that with our friends and families.

So we trudged on, getting on with life.

Some of us were lucky—the armor faded, developed cracks and eventually fell away in big and little chunks.

Helped by family and friends, it lost its usefulness.

But some of us weren't as lucky and are still wearing that armor 40 or 50 years later.

Not having been able to let go, not having been able to lighten the load,

some of us may carry that burden to our graves.

But maybe some of us will get lucky and finally be able to drop the heavy load and step out into the sun,

to feel the warmth on our face.

To have the load shared and lifted by those in a similar place, those around us who care.

Threshold: Fall 1969 by Warren Dupree

Homeward bound on a great circle course. We rounded the northern coast of Luzon, Philippines, and headed on a course of 060 degrees at 15 knots.

I relieved the quartermaster of the watch to stand mid-watch, which is midnight to 0400 hours. Complete and total darkness with no moonlight for visual navigation. Working with the radar repeater all I could get was a range and bearing, and after an hour of this I was getting desperate to get a solid navigational position off the land mass and three small islands.

I took the parallel motion protractor and drew a straight line to connect the range and bearings of the past hour.

Taking a close look at the line drawn on the ship's chart, I saw it centered on a small island mass to our north. "Oh, my god!"

The water depth was over 700 fathoms, but our ship's fathometer showed the bottom was coming up fast. "Not good!"

We were within minutes of running aground.

I shared this with our office-of-the-deck on watch and advised a course change.

The ocean was pushing the ship's heading from 060 degrees to 030 degrees in a more northerly direction. The ship's captain was awakened and came to the bridge. Only he could order a course change at that time.

The feelings of desperation really kicked in hard with a thirteen-thousand ton ship and over three hundred crew members' safety my full and complete responsibility.

Ship's captain ordered a course change based on my recommendation, and saved me the nightmare of a court martial and certain prison time.

During that midwatch, I went from a nineteen-year-old seaman to an old salt in a matter of moments. I realized I had full and complete responsibility for the safe navigation of a fighting man-of-war and crew.

My life changed forever!

I crossed a threshold, never to return as life was before, my midwatch duties.

What I Carried by David Robinson

What I carried growing up . . .
Water, wood, milk bucket, slop bucket, corn and hay, saw, axe, fear if I
didn't get my work done before dad got home, then it'd be a whoopin' I'd
carry.
Love for my family, honor for my parents. Deep respect for my country
and my father who'd fought in WWII and Korea. Obedience to those in
authority, dislike for school. Hate for my dad's drinking, his medicine for
what we now call PTSD.

What I carried in Vietnam . . .
    A New Testament my sister gave me, a rucksack containing a
poncho, poncho liner, c-rations, three canteens of water, heat tabs, bug
juice, M16, seven magazines of ammo plus extra, at least 100 rounds
of M60 ammo, four hand grenades, the ammo box containing writing
paper, pen, envelopes, billfold and pictures.
    Hate from being away from home, hate for the monsoon rain,
skeeters, leeches, booby traps, firefight, snipers . . . hate for anyone who
wouldn't watch out for their buddy.
    And hate, fear, regret, sorrow and a sickening feeling when
seeing or hearing the horrifying words: "he got it." And the worst of all:
"he didn't make it."
    Fear of all the things I hate, then there's the sad and glad. Glad
I'm going home, but so sad my brothers aren't going with me. And the
heaviest load of all: "if I had of."

What I carried back home . . .
Gladness to be back, sadness about the brothers still there, madness the
way all our heroes were treated. . . disgust, rage, hate, sorrow . . . ashamed
of the people who thought more of a draft-dodging-coward than of a
brave, fighting and willing soldier.

Respect and honor for all those that served and are still serving. Remembrance for all who died with loving, thankful and honoring memory.

And PTSD that no one could see . . .

What I carried but didn't know
When you looked at me it didn't show
I kept quiet so it would go
But it stayed inside my head twirling and twirling
Sometimes even wishing I was dead
You're the one to blame
You should bear all the shame
I had no idea why it would be so
Why does it keep terrifying me
Oh please just let me be
How could you handle what you can't see?
All these years I thought it was just me
But my brothers said no, it's PTSD

Final Exam by David Rozelle

The morning sick call line was led by Billy James. Bill was a meek, undersized, 18-year-old PFC who served as a rifleman in the 1st Squad of Bravo Company, 8th Brigade, First Cavalry Division. The unit was headquartered a few doors west of our aid facility. For the two weeks leading up to this morning, his squad had been involved in some heavy combat situations. The unit was an air mobile unit of the "bring you in when fighting is really bad and we need more guns" kind of unit. When times were good they spent most of their time training a few hours a day and then hanging out at the PX or one of the many continuous card games on base. The last month their card games had been shorter than usual and the 1st squad had been emptying a lot of ammo boxes.

Billy was never a rock star soldier. He would take any opportunity or reason to avoid a flight to a gun fight so we knew him pretty well. His medical file was easily the thickest we had in our facility. In the two weeks of his squad's heaviest action Billy had been an early morning regular. We knew his history and knew his unit was on base. He came to my desk with the same general symptoms and with the same pitiful attitude. He said he was sick all over and had a fever and just had no energy.

As a human being Billy was not of the angry, cursing, demanding type. I never heard him say or heard of him saying we were "treating him unfairly" or "picking on him." We had tested everything; we had equipment to check and our best medical doctors had physically checked him. At this point we were, as a medical body, convinced Billy was a garden variety "Gold Brick" kind of soldier. Following the visit Billy had paid us just two days ago we had called his Platoon leader in and explained that we could find no reason he should not be returned to duty. The highest-ranking doctor of our unit had signed papers to that effect and we washed our hands of the affair.

Billy showed a lot of persistence and ability to absorb abuse coming back to see us again and for that reason alone I took some blood from him along with the blood pressure, pulse, respiration and temperature routine for such visits. When everything turned up normal I sent him back to his unit.

The morning went routinely for an hour or so; then the medical tech walked in. He had just finished the blood work up on one Billy James and Billy was positively suffering from malaria.

The work staff held a short meeting and decided since I was the medic who last treated Billy, it was only fair that I take the news to him and his commanding officer. Ever the good little soldier and the low-ranking member, I picked up the revised paperwork and headed west to Billy's company headquarters. The Top Sergeant was not happy to see me or my news, but he quickly got word to Billy's squad leader to replace him and send him to headquarters.

I stood around uncomfortably in the dust and heat of the headquarters office, expecting to have a long wait. I was surprised as Billy appeared almost immediately. The company was in their jeep and ready to leave for the land strip and Billy got what he called a stay of execution. I explained what had happened and that we needed him back at our treatment facility to start meds and hospitalization immediately. He did not seem surprised and gave me the "I told you I was sick" look.

I got Billy signed into the ward just in time to make it to the mess hall before last call. The cook squad pushed me hard to finish so they could get out of the kitchen. I rushed through the mystery meat of the day and went back to the treatment facility.

The rest of the day was uneventful. I got a couple of surgical packs sorted, swept the floor a few times and read an interesting chapter of the Merck Manual concerning antibiotic treatment for urinary tract infections. Just before evening chow a medivac chopper came in and dropped us a gunshot victim. The poor soldier was showing a newbie how to safely clean an M-16 rifle when it discharged a round through his right foot. It took very little time to clean it up and send him off to the bigger hospital. As I was leaving for chow the company clerk met me and walked to mess with me. It was rare that he came to the treatment facility but I had known him training in Texas so it did not strike me as unusual.

Once we were seated, the clerk surprised me. He had just gotten paperwork that I was listed to process out of country the next morning and to report to Buen Hoa airport by late the next afternoon in preparation for returning home. My short timer calendar still showed two weeks before I was due to leave. We made small talk, ate our meal and made plans for me to meet him at the company headquarters at 1900 hours to start the paperwork. I do not remember eating anything.

For an undertaking as complicated as moving a soldier from a military unit to another and then miles and miles to his home, the paperwork required was child's play. My clerk handed me a single sheet of paper with a listing of the company subsection spelled out and a block at the far right side of the paper that the boss of department initialed saying I had turned in all the equipment I borrowed, used, eaten of theirs. I knew the head of each branch and quickly ran each down and had them initial my paper. The medical was a bit more involved but since I usually performed the physical for each of the men leaving, I did a windshield evaluation, filled in the blanks, initialed the sheet and moved on. In less than thirty minutes I had the papers complete with the necessary autographs and back to the clerk's office. He was to get the commanding officer's approval the next morning and I would be good to go.

I did not even pretend I would be able to sleep. I packed up all the things I wanted to take home with me and they filled only the bottom of my duffel bag. I dumped a clean pair of underwear, a pair of socks and a Merck Manual I had rescued from book heaven. The remaining hoard I got in a heap between my bunk and the hutch door. I can't remember a complete inventory, but there were a few under pants and shirts which had never been worn. There was a pair of jungle boots which were highly polished and never worn. There were at least two sets of fatigue uniforms, still in the condition they came from supply. I had a stack of books I had traded or borrowed against hard times. The stash included a reel to reel tape recorder which I had inherited from a roommate who did not want to take it home with him and other treasures of equal value.

When morning broke I dressed smartly and sat on my bunk numbly until I could hear daily life outside the hootch. I went out to breakfast and ate quickly. I was aware that I was not included in the chatter of the morning but not alive enough to think anything of it. I shuffled back to my little room and found my roommates had gone to their duty stations without me. I methodically marshalled my worldly possession to the left side of my hootch door, gathered up my near empty duffel bag and necessary paper work and walked toward the office without looking back.

At the company office my clerk friend took the remaining indispensable papers to the Commanding Officer who signed them without comment or glance to see who it was for and I was ushered out the door and told to meet the resupply helicopter which was to be leaving for Ben Hoa shortly. I knew it would be half an hour easily before departure and thought I would like to see the treatment facility one last time so I walked the short hill where it was planted.

Sick call was over for the morning and the crew was cleaning the treatment room and discussing the morning's events. I walked through the door expecting some congratulations, good luck speeches, *we'll sure miss you around here*, or some social banter. No one seemed to notice I was there. I walked a bit closer to the action and shuffled my feet a little but still got no reaction. At this point I figured the guys were playing with my mind and if I turned to leave they would bring me back and give the old family send off. So I turned and walked slowly towards the door and the now-awaiting resupply helicopter. There was no comment and when the helicopter was in the air and the company area out of sight I was left with the feeling of just having attended my own funeral.

One of These Boots by Gabriel Garcia

Memorial Day 2015 was the first Memorial Day for me since coming home from Afghanistan. These were my thoughts when I saw thousands of boots on a football field in Fort Bragg, NC. Each boot had a small American flag along with an I.D. tag of the photo, name, and date of when that Service Member died overseas. There were over 20 boots from the day I left the United States in December 2013 to the day I returned home safely in August of 2014. Thousands of names, stories, pain, and tears are on these boots. This poem is dedicated to every Soldier, Marine, Airmen, Sailor, and Coast Guardsmen that are one of these boots.

A flag, a photo, a name, and a date are all on one boot.

A memory, a story, a laugh, and a cry are all on one boot.

A son, a husband, and a friend are all on one boot.

A daughter, a sister, and a nurse are all on one boot.

A hero, a Medal of Honor recipient, a book, and a movie are all on one boot.

A crew, a team, a crash, and a tragedy are all in a group of boots.

A son of a Command Sergeant Major, a Samoan family in their traditional attire and art are all displayed on one boot.

A husband who transferred bases to be with his wife on Christmas, who was killed two days later is on a boot.

A highly decorated Airborne Ranger with over 30 years of military service and multiple combat deployments is on a boot.

A 2-Star General who was killed in an insider attack is on a boot.

Two Paratroopers killed in an insider attack within days of arriving in country are on a pair of boots.

A Senior Enlisted Paratrooper who went home in a flag-draped coffin and placed on the back of a C-17 cargo plane is on a boot.

A Paratrooper who volunteered for another tour so that his fellow comrades could spend time with their families is on a boot.

Seeing the names, faces, and dates that were on these boots made me realize that I could have been one of these boots.

Mission by Monica Blankenship

August 2021.

Kabul has fallen. Chaos, desperation, terror, death. The frantic evacuations, the attempts to get out. The graphic picture of a baby being handed over barbed wire to a Marine by a begging mother.

Like a gut punch to memory. The babies.

April 1975.

It's finally going to be over. Saigon has fallen. Frantic, desperate attempts to get out.

I am less than a year in the AF, a 2nd Lt. Nurse coming off night shift at DG Medical Center, Travis AFB, Women's Surgery. As I prepare to head home my friend Connie, coming on to days, and I are notified that we were being reassigned temporarily to AES (Air Evac Staging Facility). Report there the next morning. Made sense, lots of troops coming through Travis in those days.

The next morning there they were. The babies. The littlest from the experience of Saigon, in their cardboard box beds, needing everything.

Operation Babylift. It began April 4, 1975. The humanitarian US attempt ordered by Pres. Ford to evacuate as many as possible from the emptying frightened orphanages of Saigon. C-141's, C5's already hauling troops began bringing the children over the Pacific. These troops held these babies for take offs and landings and for many of the long flight hours, caring for them along with the flight medical staff assigned.

In AES we worked long hours: bathing, feeding, treating the myriad of what needed to be treated. And holding and comforting as we could. And then the guys coming into the unit as they were leaving Travis; they came to hold and say "Goodbye" to 'their' babies...the ones they had held for those long hours. Little "Mai Tai" as she was named by her soldier, smiling in the arms of her guy, crying again as he left. And the tears they tried to hide, and my tears, watching. Those were the pictures never taken, but locked in my mind.

No, not the work that drained, but the emotion. The in-your-face impact of the war's reality in our safe corner of the world. We saw it, of course, in the faces and manner of the troops coming back, and dealt with that on one level; but this, this was different for me. These children, not AP pictures but in my arms, some truly war orphans; some, yes, Amerasian, fathered by an American and given up by a young Vietnamese girl; some thrust at American personnel by parents begging to get their child to safety, to a better life.

There were many flights in those crazy days of Operation Babylift, civilian and military. Each with their own story. Over 2000 orphans were rescued and eventually found new homes. But there is at least one story that needs telling here...

The first flight on April 4. The C-5 that didn't make it to Travis, or even to the Philippines. With over 300 on board it crashed shortly after takeoff, when a cargo door burst open at 23,000 ft. 128 died, 78 of them children. A nurse I later met very briefly was the Medical Crew Director for that flight, and only survived because she had just left the cargo area to retrieve medication upstairs. Though significantly injured herself, she among others repeatedly crawled back into a burning plane in a rice paddy to pull as many children and troops out they could. I was so in awe of her as I later became a flight nurse myself, flew many long Pacific Theater hours as crew director, and realized the magnitude of what she and those people were dealing with at that time.

So, where do I go with this story now? Maybe this is titled wrong. Maybe "Innocent Victims?" Maybe "The Babies?" I don't know.

In remembering these "victims," I see again other victims I saw during that time as a nurse. The young troops we had as patients with their debilitating physical injuries, emotional and psychological trauma that led to enormous substance abuse, loneliness, isolation in their communities. Those that could never find "normal" again, those that died in our care. The medical staff that tried, fought it with them, that burned out.

It was a grasping of the reality of the war, maturing in a military and emotional world of a country coming to grips with failure...its pain, futility, courage, humanity...its innocence, its malevolence. Did this effort of Operation Babylift console us? Did we appreciate the tenderness, the toughness of all involved? Did these little faces bring us resolve?

This is what Kabul brought back to me. Overwhelming remembering, tears, and questioning a world where it continues to happen. I now have children of my own who have been in Afghanistan, Iraq and now have one heading to Ukraine. An old friend, a Jesuit priest that spent over 50 years in India and Nepal, said to me once that "Mothers should run countries."

I believe him.

Where I am From by Ron Kuebler

Beginnings are hard to remember
They tell me Allentown, P.A., was near
I tell people I was born in the south
And spirited away to P.A., close your mouth
It doesn't really matter that much
I grew and grew to a man as such
Went to Cleveland to learn about ocean
And studied metals as a predilection
Failed that but the Army beckoned
It was in the stars I reckoned
Did my tour in Vietnam one year
Came back to USA with a bent ear
Studied metals once again and met
The girl who lost my money on a horse bet
Started a company up in the north
It went south and I ventured forth
Played with ice cream and lost my shirt
Studied speech therapy and donned a skirt
Finally found myself in a company started
Taught them to speak and then parted
Three boys who all became eagles
Flew apart like a bunch of seagulls
The pride I feel is tantamount
To the spray I feel from the fount

No Escape by Ray Crombe

There was a twenty-one-year period of life after Vietnam when I would have said that things were fine, and all was under control. What I didn't realize though was that there really is no escape. PTSD can only be held at bay – but not stopped. Pain demands to be heard – and heard it will be. Even when we think we have locked it safely away, as I look back – I can see that it was subtly directing and guiding my life and decisions.

Besides work, wife, two kids, a dog, cat and a white picket fence, I felt driven to fill something that was missing still. I volunteered in a dozen areas, all demanding much of my time and energy, causing loss of attention to my family. Trying to fill a void that I didn't even understand or know existed. The compartments of my mind that all of Nam stuff was stuffed away into were leaking, and I didn't comprehend it. But it was yelling – "There is No Escaping."

But then – yes, one specific minute of one specific day, standing at the end of the driveway of a house we were moving to, it seemed as though a dump truck silently backed up to me and emptied its entire load of terror and confusion on me all at once. I felt buried. So, what is all this? Hours and hours of tears. Where did my appetite go? I can't function at work although I have been doing the job for twenty years. Weak and vulnerable so instantaneously, and for unknown reasons. Clueless. Pain that would be not only mine, but will spread out in waves and then ripples to my family and to many others.

Injuries had occurred back there – moral injuries – that now scream to be addressed and to be healed. Can't just ignoring the problem cause it to go away? Not think about it, and all will be well - right? Is there no easy way of escape? The next four years were awful.

Thoughts, memories, situations, would now keep coming back. Failures, regrets, losses, helplessness, so many things that went on – things that we said at the time "Don't Mean Nothin." But as we suspected they truly did mean something. I guess we needed to deal with it all by not dealing with it. Easier to avoid it – or so we thought.

I cried for hours, and still cry for those vets who have also grieved (and grieved much worse), those who paved the way with continued suffering so the military would eventually recognize that PTSD was a real thing and needed attention. Cried for those who lost loved ones, for those who lost relationships, for those who surrendered dreams and experienced both loss of hope and of innocence. Oh – how far the ripples reach.

For so many years, placing stronger and stronger locks on the "protective" Vietnam compartments of my mind – proved weak and inescapable, as all of the locks gave way at once.

It was a long road back, and for so long, I thought the suffering was deserved – the warranted consequences of poor choices. I instinctively knew that Justice is getting what we deserve. Then found out that Grace is getting God's Goodness – which we don't deserve. But for which I – for one – am eternally grateful.

Vietnam's Little Political White Lies by Gerry Nieters

Little white lies usually carry the connotation of being little mistruths of little significance. As far as I'm concerned there were no little white lies in Vietnam. The whole damn encounter was a gigantic, monumental, big fat lie. We were part of the largest cluster fuck of the 20th century. There was nothing little about it. It was a war propagated by politicians and thrust upon us soldiers. We were but expendable pawns on someone else's chess board, with no individual significance except to ourselves.

No Snow Over There by Bruce Turek

snow in buffalo
six feet deep
seems a long, long way away
and don't matter much, do it.

watching august heat-shimmering waves
from chemical barrels
gives you shivers.
snow in buffalo
don't matter at all.

trembling and drenched while cold wet saw grass
cuts at your cheek
crossing the creek
don't change much
if the snow in buffalo is
six feet deep.

you are cold over there
at a hundred-three degrees
without snow at all.
even at six foot deep in buffalo.

the coldest it can get
over there in the bush,
ten thousand miles away from snow in buffalo
oozes out of his lifeless eyes
while you cradle him tight in your lap.

nothing in the world is icier
than the cooling body of one of your own.
grinched tears dropple his face
even if snow in buffalo
is six foot deep.

then it matters.

Introduction to the Field by Alan Brett

As I flew into Tan Son Nhut airport in 1967, the airport was under attack so we diverted to Ben Hoa AFB and were taken to the 90th Replacement Battalion in Long Binh. It was getting late, they showed us to our billet, and told us they were serving chow. When I returned to our billet, there was a note on my bunk saying to go to the orderly room after morning chow with all my gear.

First thing in the morning I and several other men formed in front of the orderly room. We were told that we were going to the 25th Infantry as soon as the three-quarter ton truck arrived. Fifteen minutes later we were off to the 25th. Two hours later we arrived, dusty and dirty from the trip.

I was dropped off in front of an orderly room. As I reported in, I was told that I was part of Bravo Company, 2nd of the 14th Infantry, 25th Division at Cu Chi. I was being assigned to the 1st platoon. The clerk took me over to the location of the hooch. He told me to drop my gear, go to supply and pick up a weapon, ammo and field gear, then report to the office. I did as I was told. As I was putting my gear together, the First Sergeant came out and said, "As soon as the others get here, you're going out to meet up with the company." Shortly, the others started to show up. When all five of us were there the clerk came out and said to go to the helo pad and get on the supply chopper. He also said, "Welcome to Vietnam."

The trip wasn't very long and as we got close, the door gunner told us to lock and load, that we're going into a hot LZ. As we got close, we could hear gun fire. As the chopper landed, a Sergeant ran over with some men and said that the new guys should come with him and the others should unload the supplies. We ran with him and were introduced to the Company Commander. Three others Sergeants showed up and we were assigned to each. I was introduced to my Sergeant by the CO saying stick with him; he will teach you the ropes since he's been here for eighteen months.

During all this, there were bullets flying around. We started to run toward the fighting. We jumped behind a fallen tree and my Sgt told me to shoot toward the front. All our men were on either side of us. I started to shoot and several minutes later a bullet whizzed between us, we glanced at each other, then continued firing. I glanced over toward the Sgt in time to see him slump over. I crawled over to him, saw that he was shot, and I immediately called for a medic. I took off his pot and half of his head was gone. The only thing the medic said was "the bullet had his name on it" and moved on to another wounded man. All I could think was, he's going to show me the ropes?

As I continued to fire, but after a while the fight was over and we moved back to the perimeter. I got to meet the others in the platoon. The CO said to another NCO in the platoon that he is now the Platoon Sgt. That night I was placed on a listening post, the next night I was sent on ambush patrol, and the next day as the company moved out, I was placed on point- all of which are the consequences of being the new guy. The platoon Sgt also said now you've been indoctrinated; you are now the new squad leader. After I asked him why me and he said that I was the senior Cprl on the squad, and a week later I was a Sgt E5.

What I learned from this experience was that if the bullet has your name on it, it will find you. The other thing I realized was that I had to accept death. I probably was not going to make it. This somehow released my fear of dying. I was still afraid, but it didn't paralyze me. This allowed me to do my job.

Thirty-five months later, as I got on the plane to go home, I was actually surprised that I had lived.

Coming out of the Treeline by Donna Culp

Owning a home in the Western North Carolina mountains always provided our family a much anticipated break in the routine of life. More importantly, it was the buoy to keep swimming toward for retirement. Once retired, and living in the tree line on the mountain full time, that respite took on a much deeper meaning. Finally able to claim the days as my own, the decompression from a lifetime of the work-a-day treadmill began. However, so did the unpacking of boxes chock full of mementos of a lifetime of raising a family, travel, and living abroad with the military, and the Federal Government.

Over time there was the usual purging of things that were no longer needed, or no longer held enough meaning to retain. Eventually the boxes containing reminders of my time in the military surfaced, only to get shoved into the corner. As if transported back in time, I was remembering. Recalling, as if my life was on video tape and somehow the rewind button had been pushed.

Files containing Letters of Appreciation, Letters of Recommendation, TDY and PCS orders, pay, my NEO (Noncombatant Evacuation Operations) Kit, and more. None of this had been touched since I left the military, but I held on to it in case it was needed for some unforeseen requirement. One notebook kept finding its way to my gaze. The notebook that contained the details of a chapter of my life in the military that was the source of actual nightmares. Reminders shared with a VA counselor for three years with the goal of making the night terrors stop. Encouraged by my counselor to submit a package to the VA to determine a disability rating, only to be met with denial. WTF!!!! .... Over....

What was the purpose of reliving everything only to be told that although I now carried a diagnosis of PTSD and all that entails, it didn't matter and neither did I. Having been diagnosed with PTSD didn't automatically provide resolution to the issues I had been living with. Like being diagnosed with cancer, that doesn't automatically endow the patient with all knowledge about their cancer. The diagnosis only began to identify things about myself I recognized, didn't understand, and didn't know how to fix on my own.

As always, and regardless of where I was in my head, life had to continue. Children to care for. Hold a job and keep body and soul together. Keep the household going. Some days hanging on by a thread, dreading for evening to fall, dreading the need to go to sleep. Afraid of going to sleep. Praying that God would grant me solace in slumber so I would have the mental and physical energy to get through another day. Somehow holding it together to smile, engage with my patients, coworkers, family, and friends. Feeling like I was masquerading as a fake human. What had I become? Where in the depth of my being did my soul take a turn to such darkness that I feared for my mortal life? Would the night terrors become so vivid that I would die in my sleep? Where would that leave my family?

Time passed. Children raised and on their own. After retiring from twenty-three years in the medical field, and a second career with the Federal Government, it was time to move to the mountain. Once and for all, retired.

Now living in the tree line with time and space to reflect, I sit still. Turn my ear to the gentle breeze and listen as it stirs the leaves on the trees. Lift my face to the sun. Reach my hand to the soil I'm sitting on and feel the texture of all that I touch. For the first time in my life, I am listening to my own breathing. Then there's my heartbeat. Giving myself the gift of self-validation, I acknowledge I have come through a lot and am still alive. Feeling like I'm being embraced by life in the tree line, I could sit here forever.

Living on a mountain among the trees and wildlife, A I began to realize there is nurture amongst the nature. Mother earth is giving me permission to slow down, breathe, and learn from her what I need to thrive in this new chapter of my life. The routine of life didn't really change as the basics of everyday living continued. Laundry, cooking, cleaning, and such remained constant. Gradually, creativity sparked when working to transform the area around our house into flower beds designed to attract pollinators.

Eventually I find myself connecting with life beyond the tree line. Church, veterans' organizations, and connecting with veterans like myself. Friendships, socialization, support for one another. Community. We are our own tribe. Validation. Nobody understands us like we do. There really is life beyond the tree line.

The VA says to us, don't be discouraged by being denied a claim. We too are growing, learning, and transforming the way we see you, and are striving to do better at meeting your needs. We are encouraged to go see our local VSO. Give the VA another chance to hear our story and review our claims.

Admitting to myself that I have unfinished business with the VA, the boxes, and notebook holding the details of a chapter of my military life get pulled out of the dark recess of the closet. It's unsettling to look at this again, and so initially with trembling hands, I begin to dig through it all. Then I ask myself if I really want to do this again? Risk rejection again. Then I come across a quote by some unknown author, "Positive people are not positive because they've skated through life. They're positive because they've been through hell and decided they don't want to live there anymore."

Taking a deep breath, I pick up my cell phone and schedule an appointment with my VSO, and the process begins again with the VA.

This time it isn't about the night terrors. It's about unfinished business. Medical issues. Gaining a better understanding of PTSD. My PTSD. Will all this reopen old wounds and the night terrors return? I don't know the answer, but I want to see if the VA is the place where coming out of the tree line is worth the effort.

Fight for Freedom by Ron Kuebler

I want to be free and I am
Many have given their lives like a ram
Butting our heads without thinking ahead
Just thinking it's the
right thing even if dead
Others can live as we all want to
Free to be alive and love who
We want to grow with our life
Enjoy the things everyone wants for their wife
And all around us mayhem continues
But we can enjoy our favorite menus
Freedom is not cheap and thank you for your sacrifice
You risk your life sometimes depending on the throw of the dice
Know that I and many thank you from our heart
Even though from this Earth you did part.

It's Today by Tommy Cannon

While you listen to this, I ask you to remember one name. One name of so many Brothers and Sisters, who have fallen in the name of Freedom.

Memorial Day is a day to remember the brave men and women who sacrificed everything for their brothers and sisters, and the country we love.

Names like: Gary Collins, Mark Vasquez, Joe Lister, Ryan Young, and Jarrod Black might be just another name to most.

These men are my brothers, and have paid in full for you and everyone else in this country.

Joe Dunigan, Chris Hill, Chris Ramirez, Daniel Shepherd, and John Tipton are more names for you to remember.

These men died for us while living in terrible conditions during some of the most brutal fighting in Iraq.

There are no words to describe men like Charles Price, Jacob Molina, or Craig Gaglia.

These are the best of men among men. They have laid down their lives so the people of this great nation can enjoy the wonderful freedoms generations have fought to earn and preserve.

The names of Brian Hall, Gary Woods, Jason Pautsch, Edward Forrest, and Bryce Gautier will slip your mind after hearing their names called, but never forget their purpose, and never forget their sacrifice.

We honor them not just on Memorial Day but every day, by remembering what they have done out of love for you and the freedoms that flourish within our borders.

We should all fight for the men like Michael Volfe, Heath Shubert, Nathan Smith, Adam Sines, Christian Hill, Nikolas Timmins, and Dan Filzen who left the war but it never left them.

They left this earth too early. The 22 Veterans a day who take their own lives is 22 too many.

All of these Heroes deserve to be remembered. I am here with my family everyday because of their sacrifice. You are able to be free, pray, protest, and choose the life you want because of these men, and countless others. These men are my brothers, and I thank them for what they have done for us. I will never forget them, I miss them every day, and I will always honor them with my love and my life.

Silent Bang by Theron Russell

Silence is one of the best ways a person could describe PTSD
But it is only silence for you because it is not silence to me.
It is like having a loaded gun that is placed to the back of my head.
You never hear it, but in middle of the night it wakes me in my bed.
No one else hears my agony, my heart goes thump, thump as my chest gets tight
And not a soul hears my cries, and I try to tell myself it'll be all right.
Some cheer and some stare at me but all see it on me like a face tattoo
There goes another U.S. veteran and now they wonder "what did I do."
So, even the happy ones, look down or away, they don't want to see me
Because they know in my pain they have a share, are part of my history.
Because for their right, had to fight, but at night, pray for light, as I am about to ignite and explode, from the stories untold.
And there is this war inside me on that battlefield it still rages
For "freedom" this is what I paid, my heart, soul, and mind these are the wages.
But I do not speak about these things I cannot at least never out loud
Though I wish I could say it, give it sound, just to tell the entire crowd
I wish I could just stand on a podium and share my entire heart
If all my silence I could just break, to give it a voice, that would be a start.
But I know in front of others the minute my very voice I should raise
They would strike me down and say that I am just crazy and that label stays
I wish that someone would try to understand what the silence is about
What if I did It? What if I raised my voice what if I did scream and shout?
Could they begin to hear, all my fear, see the tear, or would they jeer, as they peer into my soul, my voice to control.
So, I sit here in my silence and wonder if that is how it will end.
More veterans have died from suicide than war and that's the truth my friend.

Still the news channels are silent, worried about some movie star I guess.
Stars can get more ratings than saving a vet, that's how it works with the press.
It does not, and will not change that simple fact, that by this same time tomorrow
About 20 more of my brothers or sisters, GONE. I feel that sorrow.
The real question for you, will you ignore the truth and all of this science?
Or will you stand up, speak up, interrupt, and help us to break the silence?
So, will it be you who sings into my heart the song that needs to be sang?
Or in the darkness, will the last sound that breaks my silence be Click, CLICK! (bang)

Packing by Frank Cucumber

I packed all the knowledge from basic training first in the duffel bag. Then, my military clothing, a small bag of personal things, shaving kit, a set of civvies for a change off duty. On top of that was all the excitement to learn the trade of heavy equipment, then after that, putting my new knowledge of training and the excitement of going, and wondering what was waiting for me in Vietnam.

Now the bag is full.

Locked up and ready to go.

Smells by Steve Henderson

As a child I remember that smells meant so many different things to me, some good, some bad. I remember certain perfumes smelled so good to me and others were distasteful. The first bad smell I remember was going home on the school bus one day, and there was a lady in her front yard surrounded by firemen. She had been burned badly while burning leaves. This was the worst odor I had ever smelled. I did not know it, but years later this smell returned in Viet Nam thru Napalm and other war time casualties. It would linger in your nose for a long time.

I remember when I went down to the induction center in Charlotte the night before I joined the Marine Corps. The old musky smell of the hotel room I was put in, before being sworn in the next morning and leaving for Parris Island. I got up the next morning using an unfamiliar soap that even today reminds me of the day I was sworn into the Corps. I remember arriving at Parris Island in the middle of the night, stepping off the bus and smelling the early November air, very different than anything I had ever smelled before, even at the beach. Being put into tight quarters with so many other people were smells I will never forget. I remember standing in formation so long that recruits would piss or shit themselves because they were not allowed to go to the head. This was all part of the process and the smells.

I remember the smell of spit shining shoes and heating the polish and cleaning my weapon over and over again.

I even remember the smell of graduation, putting on the new dry-cleaned uniform and our new dress shoes and each item of clothes I put on that day, enhanced by the excitement of graduation.

I remember the huts we stayed in at Camp Geiger in the infantry training and the stoves that used fuel oil and the odor they gave off. Outside smelled so much different there with all the firing ranges, guns fired and the smoke that resulted.

I remember going to MOS school that was anti-tank weapons and firing the 106 recoilless rifle. I remember going to the course where we learned how to use the flame thrower. It took kerosene oil. As we went on to use Napalm and the distinct smell it gives. The smell of TNT charges going off.

I remember graduating demolition school, the smells of the depth cord as it ignited from the blasting cap…the different smell of C4. The use and the smell of TNT when exploding is like no other.

When I landed in California for survival training, the smells changed tremendously. The dry air while out in the field was completely different than anything I had smelled before. The cooking of the small pygmy rattlers was new to me. Eating vegetation that we were taught to live off, had unique smells.

On my way to Viet Nam, we stopped in Okinawa to take shots and some guys got sick…this smell was unbearable at times. Stepping of the plane in 100 degree heat filled your nostrils up with negative smells, all different for this North Carolina man.

When I landed in Vietnam and stepped off the plane, I was not ready for the 120 degree heat I was taken back by the smell of the burning of human waste. There came my first day in the bush, the smell of the jungle, the heat, the smell of grunts in the same clothes for months and then the smell of death of the enemy, of our casualties was undeniable.

When I was medi-vaced to Guam it was a smell of Vietnam and the smells I had left behind with my family. When I arrived at the hospital I was placed on a ward with mainly amputees. The wounds were not closed so there were so many smells of the dying flesh. When the wounds were cleaned in the morning, the smell got stronger. It was very unpleasant but better than the alternative of death for me.

When I arrived back in the United States in Alaska, the temperatures changed by about 80 degrees. When I finally got home, the smells of my family, my community, my home smelled just like it did the day I left. It was so good to be home.

Today I am reminded of these smells in certain situations. The smells were part of the experience, making it more vivid and more distinguishable.

The Year 1990—Mentor by Stacie Litsenberger

His large hand of an unspoken life clenched my 22-year-old hand as we slowly walked in silence. The year was 1990. I was an American Soldier who was befriended by his daughter to join their family for Christmas Eve dinner as my friends and husband had already deployed to the Persian Gulf from Germany. We made our way over cold generations of hand-hewn cobblestones as snow ever so lightly fell. I remember his thick black wool coat as I felt he was like a bear trying to protect me. We reached the German village, and in the darkness of midnight, reached a small church lit only by candlelight.

We sat on Bavarian worn church pews that could handle any burden, any joy. We sat in silence as prayers and wishes of Christmas joy went unheard by us. This man whom I just met hours earlier during Christmas Eve dinner, a World War II Veteran who survived as a German soldier and as prisoner of war in Russia began to quietly say, "Krieg ist shlecht, krieg ist schlect," war is difficult, war is difficult. His hand continued to clench mine, giving me each hope that I would not experience his own memories and terror of the combat of men. I trembled a little from the cold and more from my own thoughts as I knew the next day—I too would be forever changed as a young US Army Soldier off to my generation's war.

Nha Trang by Bruce Turek

On an occasional day off, I'd chopper from the field into Nha Trang to
go to the Pony Bar
on Nguyễn Thi Rd, almost to the beach. It was more like a
neighborhood hangout
rather than a typical soldier joint, although sometimes at night
a Saigon Tea hustler or two would show up.

Cia and her brother An worked there, along with mama-san. The kids
were about 10 and 11 years old,
each of them no taller than my thigh. Cute and energetic, but still
children,
they helped with glass washing and floor mopping and bringing me
an occasional bottle of Ba Muoi Ba; it was the rice beer labeled "33."

Cia also kept the books - very carefully and diligently. I marveled at her
young acumen.
So did her mother. She would smile at me and wink
because no words were necessary to show her pride.

In midafternoon, if there were any customers at all, two or three of us,
total, could be sitting
either at the bar or at one of the tiny tables. No music blaring, no
antagonisms, just a quiet breeze.

That was my favorite time - sunny and peaceful, with no occasional
sounds of war.
Cia and An and I talked to one another with sign language and the odd
Asian-shaped English word.

After a few visits, we got to know each other by name. I was Charlie,
pronounced "Chollie."
They were "Chaw" and "Ahn." We became buddies.

With their mom's approval, they would be allowed to let loose and be
kids, chasing one another,
or playing a hand game, wildly laughing.
It was a joy watching them play with such tragedy all around them.

I would begin to join in, eventually playing hide and seek
or rock, paper, scissors, or just talking and kidding.

I went to that place for the last time in early July, 1967, to say goodbye
and trade addresses, then left for Tan Son Nhut air base to finally fly
home to the U.S.

After about 6 months, in Pennsylvania, I got a letter from Cia, in her
neat, precise handwriting.
She and her mother were still at the bar. Her brother had been killed.
He had died stepping
on a "land bomb" in a rice paddy at his grandad's farm in the interior.
A smudge of a teardrop remained on the second page.

I was devastated, overcome with a grief equally painful as other deaths
I had known.
A mere child, caught in the crosshairs of a war with no end, with no
seen or perceived logic.
It was a despair that his sister so much wanted to share.

The double tragedy? I never answered her letter.
I lacked the emotional stamina to provide her any solace I might have
done.

Today, Tomorrow and Forever by Anne Adkins

A month after the death of our son Matthew, we received information that there was going to be a memorial service at the base in Alaska where he had been stationed for him and other service members who had been killed in the line of duty. Naturally we planned to go and were asked for our travel details prior to our arrival. We wondered about that but soon learned why. At the airport we were met by members of his unit that were his devoted friends. It was a nice surprise and we wanted to do something special to spend more time with them while we were there. We asked them for the name of a restaurant where we could all go to dinner that evening and they gave us the name of a restaurant that was Matthew's favorite and where they had raised hell and had a great time together. Sounded good to us and we made the reservation.

The ceremony itself was very difficult for us, but later, being there with Matthew's buddies living it up was touchingly sad but lovely. They drank and told us funny stories about Matthew and his antics and the good times they had had together. The party continued, but earlier I had noticed a young man there that had been very solemn and not laughing or joining in with his friends. He approached me and asked if we could please go outside. Once outside he told me his name was Craig Flannigan and he was a dear friend of Matthew's. He told me he could not have dinner with us, that he did not deserve it. Did not deserve our kindness or generosity.

I was so puzzled. What could this be about? His eyes teared and there was so much pain in them it actually hurt to look at him. He said he was a medic and when the unit left to help others that needed their support there was a new medic that was part of the group and Craig was ordered to observe him if there were injuries, but he was not to assist unless the number of casualties required it. There was a long pause and he said that when Matthew was hit, he knew it was bad. He could not leave Matthew's care to the new medic as what he was doing to help Matthew was not sufficient, he felt. He remembered he was not to help and hesitated for several minutes then against orders he jumped out of his vehicle, and took on Matthew's care himself. He was later punished for not following orders.

He then turned to me crying and said, "It's my fault he died. Don't you see? I should not have waited. I should have been able to save him. It's my fault he's dead." I could see in his eyes the desperation, panic and fear he felt when trying to save Matthew. "I didn't act soon enough to save him. It's all my fault." He was obviously broken and I told him he was not at fault and finally I was able to talk him into returning to the restaurant, but his sad demeanor continued. We continued to talk that evening and I was so concerned about his depression, guilt and agony that I was very fearful he might try to harm himself.

I called him after the event and he called me. We continued to talk and it seemed that began to help him. Eventually we bonded. It became a very close relationship. He asked us to come to Alaska to meet his wife and children and we did. Visits continued and the bond between our families deepened. We continued to visit and made several family trips together. So many good times together. The relationship continued and still does, and one day, they called and asked us to come one more time to Alaska before Craig was transferred to Colorado. We went. After all, they were like family. While we were at their apartment he grabbed my hand and asked if we could go outside just the two of us. Once there he looked at me with an expression I could not quite identify, then said: "Matthew loved you so much. He would talk about you so much and it was so obvious you two had such a special love for each other." He looked away from me at first, but then said, "I have to ask you something. I had no mother. You know that." His mother left when he was three and his father raised him, but not well at all—but that's another story. He said, "I never had a mama, but now I feel like I do. Do I? Is it ok if I call you mom? Will you sort of adopt me?" I looked down and considered his request. After several minutes of silence, I looked up, and as we looked at each other, we both had tears in our eyes. I took his hands in mine and said, "If you will adopt me as your mother. I love you too, darling. You may not have had a mother when you grew up but you do now. I am now your adopted mother and you are my adopted son." Now, today, tomorrow and forever, Matthew will never be replaced in our hearts and our grief continues, but I think we feel that the commitment we both made to each other helps us celebrate Matthew and the so, so very special son and friend he was and remains. Now, today, tomorrow and forever. Now, today and forever.

Where Flowers Never Bloom by Gerald Biggs

Some years earlier (67-69) before arriving in Vietnam, I dealt on a daily basis with the results this war had produced. Assisting with the movement of the wounded and killed through the far east back to the states. Now here I am in Vietnam, the country where no joy or beauty exist.

I eagerly crawled into my bunk. It was damp and cold from the persistent monsoon.

Rain which never seemed to stop. The smell of mold and mildew was everywhere,

even my olive-green woolen issue blanket smelled of nature's relentless deluge.

I lay there staring out through the louvered sides of my hooch at the moon,

which struggled to break through the dark cloudy sky. My thoughts raced back to my

own struggles within. Like the moon a dark shadow had captured my inner feelings

and the ability to connect with others and express myself.

There was no name or label at that time to hang on this sickness; you just dealt with it as best you could.

I have no love or compassion for Vietnam which had already caused so much pain and

permanent scarring. Maybe someday this will change. This is not the first war to produce this feeling nor will it be the last.

When the presence of constant death and mangled bodies become part of daily life it leaves

a scar and dark shadow embedded in one's memory forever. One becomes hardened and

withdrawn, living in self-imposed isolation, shutting others out, even loved ones. Now here

I am serving in the country that had already fed and propagated this feeling within me.

There is no joy in serving here, no happiness or positive influences to feed one's soul. If

you plant a flower and fail to water it and provide nourishment it will wither and die, never

producing a beautiful flower. The same is true for the soul of man. This was already the bitter

fruit of Vietnam. It's not easy living outside the norm, not being able to express your feelings,

remaining withdrawn and having frequent anxiety attacks. But this is my life now, after existing in

A country where there is no beauty to behold and where flowers never bloom.

The Call of the Wall by Gerry Nieters

The Vietnam Memorial in Washington D.C. (The Wall) was dedicated on Veterans Day, November 11, 1982. It has great significance to us Vietnam veterans. Most of us hold dear at least one name on that large subterranean polished black granite memorial, for it is truly a memorial to individuals. Many of us are both attracted to it and repulsed by it. Many of us want to go to it but do not because of all the emotions we're afraid that will come flooding back. Yes, to visit it would be good, but the pain may be greater, in fact too great. I had this very real feeling that if I went, I would start to cry, and wouldn't be able to stop.

In the Spring of 1983, I went to find one of those names. I approached the book, the directory, near the East entrance of The Wall. The directory is in alphabetic order and gives the location of the name on The Wall which is in the order of the date of death. I found the name and started to cry and walked away. That autumn I made the 400-mile journey again. This time I got to the entrance but couldn't start the decent down the walkway in front of all those names. Again, I started to cry and just walked along the top of The Wall and left.

What started as a want, now became a need. I had to return. I wanted to be there when no one else was there. On a very cold snowy Sunday morning late in January 1984, I once again stood at the entrance to The Wall in the predawn dim light. There was only one person faintly visible along the opposite wing. All my prerequisites were met. I was alone. It was quiet. The gently falling snow muffled sound. So why was I standing there unable to move forward? As the predawn early light increased, I needed to act. I needed to move. This was the place. This was the time.

I started to walk slowly along the gently descending slope arriving at panel 60. I stopped and looked at the right end of line 5. Clifford Sappleton. I began to cry and cry and cry unashamed as there was no one to see me. I was startled when I felt someone touch my shoulder. It was the man from the other side of the Memorial. He asked if I was alright. I simply pointed to the name. I cried until I ran out of tears.

Suicide by Ron Kuebler

What a word for a state of mind
We do not want to encourage
But weak we are to resist
Its hold on our psyche
Weak to leave its tenacious clutches
Strong to gather the tools of destruction
That tear apart our body and our mind
But first our body as we see death
Approaching relentlessly or quickly
So that our mental torment
Is forever gone away
Our memories that taunted us
Drained into the oblivion of nothingness.

Commitment, Community, Camaraderie by Lew Harding

In February 1966, the war seemed so distant, so remote, so impossible to find any meaning in or any reason for. We knew our squadron was going. Our aircraft carrier had been assigned to the seventh fleet in the Pacific, commanded by Admiral John McCain. We had to go. Why not make the best of it? Orders are orders. I cannot violate my oath.

When we departed the fleet landing at Mayport Naval Air Station, our sailors "manned the rail," the bands played and the tears rolled as our families waved. God be with us. How many would not come back? Would we ever see them again? Chin up, false bravado, hand salute. Now what?

I knew we had to fight. But what for? Financial markets or family members. Oh, yes, for God and country. Which God, which country? Maybe for the opportunity to demonstrate democratic ideals and our American multi-cultural diversity and freedom. That's it, freedom of expression and from oppression. That's got to be it.

I did a lot of thinking on the two-week trip from Florida, through Suez, to Subic Bay in the Philippines. As a member of a tribal community, a minority group, with a life steeped in the tragic story and reality of the "Trail of Tears" mindset, I felt conflicted. I was torn apart by the contrast of what I was doing and what I believed. Were we really going to fight for the reasons we were being told, or something else?

The first time off the catapult on Yankee Station, the commitment to do my duty spiraled into serving with a squadron of brothers and doing my best. They "watched my six" as I did theirs. Sometimes Chinese-piloted MIG-21 aircraft would dash from behind the cover of Hainan Island which was off-limits to us. As we approached the coastal city of Haiphong, they would harass and pass but never fire. Hanoi and Vinh were heavily defended. The sky always lit up with anti-aircraft fire beginning at Haiphong. We couldn't bomb the harbor at Haiphong because the State Department was concerned that we may hit one of

Aristotle Onassis' Greek cargo ships busy unloading war supplies for the North Vietnamese. Go figure.

You came to appreciate dedication and professionalism of your squadron at times like these and the feelings last for a long time. The feelings of being in a hostile fire envelope for so long in a peaked-out neurological overwhelm were sometimes followed by a desolation of spirit and the no-man's-land in between. Day after day, night after night for a month. Then south to "Dixie Station," always a relief. During our close air support for ground troops, many times fighting for their lives, we would drop cans of napalm, fire HVARS (high velocity aircraft rockets) and use 20 mm cannon fire to protect our troops. Our injuries were minimal on Dixie Station, with the exception of the la Drang Valley. Actor Mel Gibson and his Hollywood cronies made it look easy in their movie "We Were Soldiers Then." It wasn't.

The corrosive and systemic racism that I grew up with in the South left me suddenly and completely one night over Hanoi. Back on Yankee Station on a bad weather night, my wingman, a "person of color" saved my life. I am here because he was there. The best wingman a white boy could ever have screamed at me on a 242.0 Guard frequency when our strike frequency went off the line. I pulled up and off a AAA target and he yelled, "'SAM's AWAY, hard left, hard left." I was shocked, scared, and grateful all at the same time. The bright light of the missile exhaust filled my cockpit. I still feel the same way to this day, some sixty years later. The PTSD that is ever with me cannot break the bond of love and appreciation of brother saving brother over six decades ago. After an experience like that the commitment became deeply held and sharply focused. The camaraderie forged in war is an unbreakable bond, a transformative and healing power. On that dark, rainy night his desperate and timely warning helped me shift from survival to a thrival mindset for the rest of the war. The healing of old beliefs, patterns, and fears began that night that ultimately helped me in creating balance for making lifetime decisions based on gratitude. Survivor's guilt was overcome, and the giving back mission became a giving now calling. I realized that my skill and training could be useful in ways that could increase their effect and at the same time heal my wounds. The wounds which for years and years I was repressing and pretending I didn't have.

For those of you reading this who have ever dropped cans of napalm on a troop line and watched as enemy soldiers rolled on the ground to try to get the jellied gasoline off of them, you know. Some of the "troops" in black pajamas were teenagers, boys and girls. About the age of your grandchildren now. They can't pin enough colorful ribbons on your uniform to lose that memory. To you I would say the answer to your question of "Why am I still here?" is another question, "How may I serve?"

Attitude is everything. Pick a good one.

Thank you for your service. Blessings and love.

The Price of Kindness by Mike Smith

"I got the cell phone. Matt's already on the line," Sylvia said, holding it out to me.

"Hey, Matt. It's a German Shepherd – looks pretty well cared for. What do you want me to do?"

"See if you can find an entry wound."

"I already checked, and I can't see anything."

"Okay, can you move him?"

"Well, he was pretty terrified when I got here, but I got him gentled down some... Let me see."

I pushed gently on his shoulder, and the dog rolled onto his side. As he did, the loose skin on his chest moved up, and I saw it. It was a small hole in the beautiful brown-and-black coat of a dog with the long nose and proud ears of his breed.

"Found it, Matt. Entry wound on his lower chest; looks like a .22 round."

"Okay, good. Check for bleeding."

I checked.

"Dammit."

"What?"

"The wound isn't sucking, but there's blood on his lips and some coming out his nose."

"Okay, Mike. You can bring him in if you want, but all I can do is put him out of his misery."

I kept my hand on the dog's neck, stroking. When I pulled it away, he looked up at me and whimpered. I put my hand on him again.

"Matt, all that'll do is put him through another forty-five minutes of hell. I'll do it here."

"All right. If anybody objects, you can refer them to me. Sorry I couldn't help."

"Okay if I refer them to you if I find the son of a bitch who did this?" It seemed to me the shooter needed an attitude adjustment.

"I can help you out with the dog. Mike, but I have to draw the line at humans."

"Yeah. Even people who kill for the fun of it. I'm blowin' steam, Matt.'"

I said goodbye and handed the phone back to a hovering Sylvia.

"Mike, I'm sorry... I just couldn't do it," she said.

"It's okay." I talked to the dog and stroked his head and ears some, telling him about chasing balls and chewing on bones. Sylvia walked back toward her car and away from it. I told the beautiful German shepherd everything would be okay.

I pulled the trigger.

A neighbor driving past stopped and volunteered to take care of burying him. I was already staring at nothing, but I thanked Therral, and I hoped he knew I was grateful.

The next day, I rested. I sat on my top patio step overlooking the creek, and I rested. I watched the deer come to the creek, saw the leaves on the trees, the green tree line. I watched the slow progression of clouds across the sky, saw a glint of sun from a high-flying jet; the flash of light from their canopies as they rolled into dives, steep and fast. It seemed impossible that they could pull out of it, but they did, and a quarter mile of jungle would go up in napalm flames beneath them. And I looked at the trees.

We could not tell if they were fishermen or soldiers, so for our survival, they were soldiers. All of them. It mattered only that the shot was accurate when you took it, because a board and search can go to Hell in an instant. And I watched the deer drink, and I watched the Blue Heron fish in the creek.

I spent almost a week ... resting. After days, the trees on the far side of the creek seemed to become less of a tree line. After days, thoughts of the flat trajectory and heat trail of a 30-06 round faded. Slowly, I began to let go of looking at the hidden spots in the woods and assessing them as ambush sites, all the while staring at nothing.

Yes, there are things I can do that are hard, and even though I learned those things in a hellish place, I realize now there is value in them. I brought wisdom home with me, and when others might not know what to do, I can keep going. I learned to keep my head clear when it matters, knowing that I can delay paying the price until it's over.

The dog hadn't needed to spend more time alive while he slowly drowned in his own blood, and I had known the price I'd pay before I pulled the trigger. I paid it for his sake, and it was okay, because I live on twenty acres, where I can sit on my patio overlooking the creek and woods. It's beautiful here, restful and quiet.

Ask A Veteran by Ted Minnick

I returned home in July 1970. I was determined to carry on with my life without the 'demons' that others returned with. Finally, after some urging from my wife and Steve Henderson, I became a part of the "Brothers and Sisters Like These" writing alliance and have been involved for almost two years now. It's hard to put into words how much this group of brothers and sisters have meant to me. I anticipate every meeting whether I have a story to tell or not. After reading to the group in person last month I went home with another "demon" released from the closet. About two o'clock that next morning I was awakened by a thought, but it wasn't connected to any dream I was having—just a phrase. I thought about that phrase for two days before I started putting words to paper.

The next time you see a person wearing a hat bearing the words Vietnam Veteran, tell him "Thank you—Welcome Home." He might say "thank you" or "it was my honor," but be prepared for the glassy eyes, the 1000-yard stare or even tears as he tells you he has been home fifty years, and no one has ever said that to him before.

If you ask him when he was there, he might say 1968, '69, '70—but be prepared for those glassy eyes, the 1000-yard stare or maybe a tear or two as he says, "Just last night and sometimes every day."

If you ask him what he did or his MOS, he might say he was a grunt or cannon-cocker or a medic or a truck driver—but be prepared for those glassy eyes, the 1000-yard stare and maybe tears as he says what he was trained to do—kill—and he was good at his job or, he spent his days hacking through the jungle, with bleeding arms from the elephant grass, wading streams and rice paddies with leeches attached all over his body, or hunkering down in a foxhole half-filled with water during the monsoons where it rained so hard it was horizontal, sometimes scared shit-less while on guard duty, or looking and listening for the whop-whop of the helicopters coming to medevac or extract them.

If you ask him how his family is, he might say "They're good"—but be prepared for those glassy eyes, that 1000-yard stare or maybe tears as he says, "I don't know. They haven't spoken to me or reached out to me in years—they think I'm a monster who can't deal with reality or society with all of my pent-up rage and demons that no one seems to have an answer for but they sure have a name for it—PTSD—post-traumatic stress syndrome. And the doctors just prescribe another medication to take."

If you ask him where he lives, he might say Black Mountain, Asheville, or Swannanoa—but be prepared for those glassy eyes, the 1000-yard stare or a tear or two as he says in a closet or in a box under the bridge or on the street going from corner to corner and rescue missions looking for a warm blanket or a shower or a free meal—that's how he spends his days and nights.

If you ask him how he is feeling, he might say "I'm good"—but be prepared for those glassy eyes, that 1000-yard stare or maybe tears as he says his arms and shoulders hurt from swinging that machete cutting jungle or he might say his back hurts from carrying that 60-80 pound ruck filled with all his worldly possessions or his legs and knees hurt from humping that jungle up and down those central highland mountains or slogging thru those rice paddies. He might even mention that he can't hear because of the small arms fire or artillery or mortar and rocket explosions.

If you ask him if he wants a cup of coffee he might say "sure"—but be prepared for those glassy eyes, that 1000-yard stare or maybe a tear or two as he tells of hunkering under a poncho with a canteen cup full of rice paddy water, a packet of C-Ration instant coffee being heated by a piece of C-4 explosive cut out of a claymore mine, shooting the bull with his buddies who are no longer here—but he remembers all their names and where they are located on the Vietnam Veterans Memorial Wall in Washington and that they visit him every night.

You might be bold enough to ask him his age as you look at his ragged, dirty clothes, his scraggly beard and his long, oily hair and he might say 70 or 75—but be prepared for those glassy eyes, that 1000-

yard stare or maybe tears as he tells of spending his 18th or 19th birthday walking point on an ambush patrol in that same dark, triple-canopy jungle or wading those rice paddies in 100 degree heat and 100% humidity and how, during a break he and his buddies, who are no longer here, shared a small can of C-Ration pound cake drenched with a small can of C-Ration peaches or maybe a box of crumbled, smashed chocolate chip cookies that his Mom sent him. He might even mention having to eat cold chopped ham and eggs or ham and limas (frequently called ham and mothers), or scraping the congealed oil and fat out of his C-Ration beans and franks.

You might ask him when was the last time he had a bath and he might say "I don't know" or "the last time it rained," but be prepared for those glassy eyes, the 1000-yard stare or the tears as he tells of wearing his uniform and boots until they rotted off of him or stopping to rinse off in a stream with those same leeches and using a towel to dry with that hasn't been dry in weeks.

If you have this conversation with him, he might give you the short answers—but be prepared for those glassy eyes, the 1000-yard stare or the tears because you might be the only person that has taken the time to see him, to understand what he is talking about, or maybe who has lived those same horrors and experiences of combat—the one person who gets it. As you try to relate to this, consider this quote from Brian R. B. Napier: *"There is no glory in war, there is no color. There is only shadows, darkness and death. And it should be the will of all good men to find the solution whereby, no man should ever cast those shadows of death upon another."*

And you might be the one person who really wants to know and he realizes that and finally opens up about what he has been through and his life after the war—how he lived a lifetime during one year of combat in the jungles and rice paddies of South Vietnam.

So when you take the time to actually see that veteran and ask all these questions and those glassy eyes show up, the 1000-yard stare shows up or the tears begin to fall, he might finally tell the truth to someone who is the one person that has shown a genuine interest in what he has to say and what he has endured.

Richard "Boon" Preston, a friend and fellow Vietnam Veteran Brother once said *"Long after the slumber, there still be dragons."*

Thank you for allowing me to "release" another demon.

The Thing That Hurts the Most by Ray Crombe

This poem is to remember and honor one of our medics who didn't make it home, Mike Neudahl. A young eighteen-year-old kid from St. Paul who was killed while trying to aid another. Mike had a mom, dad, two brothers and a sister waiting for him to return. One Sunday morning while getting ready to leave for church, a knock on their door would change their lives forever, as life for the family would now travel downhill for all of them. Also, there was a girlfriend waiting, who was carrying his child. A child he would never get to meet, and worse yet – a child who would never get to meet his warrior dad.

Along with these feelings of sadness, are the universal ones of why him, why not me, could I have done something more that would have changed the outcome? What if this. Or what if that? If I could have done something more – and didn't – then it's my fault. Those thoughts still intrude to this day.

The things that hurt the most in life, I suspect that you may find
Are not the day to day vexations, but what we left behind.

The losses, sacrifice and battles that we fought
Woe, to find out in the end, it was all for naught.

The politicians promised that it would never be again
That next time, if there is one, we'd fight until we win.

But of course it turns out, it would be a lie
The loss of life and family's loss can only make you cry.

In The Nam our medic's gift hurt, as he walked through the door
The hurt would last forever for a life that was no more.

The only solace that maybe helps—at least there was no pain
But Little Cole, Mike could not help, so tell me, where's the gain.

The little babe that here on earth, Mike would never meet

And a child growing up without their Dad is loss of something sweet.

So on and on the ripples go, touching lives and causing hurt
The burden that the soldier carries from blood in war land's dirt.

It makes me wonder, does it end, so difficult to discern
It only ends, or so it seems, is with our Lord's return.

In honor of Specialist 4th Class, Michael L. Neudahl
Born May 22, 1951. Died Feb 4, 1970. Age 18.

Guilt by Alan Brett

I was reassigned to Battalion Headquarters and was settling in as part of the Battalion's Recon Unit. I was called to report to the Tactical Operations Center (TOC) where we were briefed on a mission. There was a company under heavy fire by the Parrots Peak on the Mekong River. I had been there about a month or so earlier with my old company. We would be choppered out and put down about four clicks East of where the company was. The team was to approach the company from the East and engage any enemy we encountered. We were told there was another team of Special Forces (SF) approaching from the North and another company from the South. Our company would be the last to arrive.

Back at our hooch, I informed the team of the mission, we grabbed our gear and went to the helo pad. A Battalion Medic was waiting and we got on the chopper that was waiting for us. The flight was short and we were put down in a small clearing. We started out pushing to the West and as we started to get closer, we could hear mortar fire off in the distance. I was surprised that we hadn't run into any enemy yet, but soon that was going to change. We were hoping to surprise the enemy and be able to engage them from their rear as they were moving toward the Company under fire. We got pinned down as we were moving and had to fight our way out and keep moving to get to the company. At first, we were hearing more fighting and the mortars and gun fire were getting louder. We were less than a click away when the gun fire started to decrease, then stop, with only sporadic shots being fired. We called in to the TOC to inform them that we were close and the gun fire had stopped. They said that they could not radio the Company CO or anyone else and to proceed with extreme caution.

As we proceeded, we came across several dead enemy. You could smell the heavy scent of gun powder lingering in the air mixed with the smell of death. We were hypervigilant, looking for any sign of an ambush or the enemy. Shortly, we came across the first American dead. They didn't have their weapons or ammo, which we thought was strange. We approached the Parrots Peak, coming in the trail from the South East, where the main body of the Company was supposed to be. We knew that the SF team was approaching from the North. They had started to see other dead, both NVA and American. We talked on the radio, giving each other our positions so we wouldn't fire on each other. As our team got to the Parrots Peak, which was an outcropping in the river, we started to see more Americans lying all over the clearing. We started to check each soldier. We did find some Americans severely wounded and unconscious, and a lot of dead. As we were checking the dead, looking for anyone that might be alive, I started to notice some of the dead were people I had served with in my previous Company. We came across the Field First Sergeant and the Company Commander from my old Company, both dead. All the ammo and weapons were gone. Our medic started attending to the wounded as we now hooked up with the SF team and then started to clear the area.

In the clearing under the trees and bushes we found a camp, a rest area for the NVA with hammocks, cook fires, and tables. It was very similar to the rest area I had come across that we had destroyed several months ago on a different operation that was in the same place. When we were there before, we had destroyed the area which now was rebuilt. The SF team had found a cache of weapons, mortars, and rockets in a nearby cave.

By now the Company that was coming in from the South started to arrive. They were going to take over the area and finish the jobs we and the SF team were doing. As we went back to the clearing where we were going to be picked up, I started to think about those dead and wounded that I knew in the company I had just left. The flight back to the Battalion area wasn't very long and the team was very quiet. We landed and I had to return to the TOC for a debriefing. This is where I found out that the company was up against a reinforced company of NVA and the Company was outnumbered two or three to one. I returned to our hooch and debriefed the team. Then we returned to cleaning our equipment and weapons. We all were going over what we had witnessed and how horrible it was. My thoughts went even further to the fact that the dead were the men I had served with just a month or so before. If I had not transferred to the Recon unit, I would have been with them and probably have died. I had a lot of trouble getting over the fact that I had left them even though I knew that I could not have done anything to change the outcome. Later, I rationalized that I had traded three years more in the military for my life. The guilt I felt has never left me. Later, after the military, I eventually started working in the Vietnam Veteran Outreach Center. Here is where I knew I could help veterans where I could not help those that I lost back then.

The One Left Behind by Dean Little

Once I packed my duffle bag, sure
I had my papers in hand to go.
Spoke words of thanks, hugs to show
bonds to those who helped me survive,
that red and green land.

Once, it took a few days travelling
From China Beach to Cam Ranh Bay
feeling guilt for the leaving, on flight
back to the world and light,
and on to home.

Once I thought I had packed me up,
all that I thought I was, before and now,
but some things were not exactly clear,
I was leaving war but not the fear,
some easiness, purpose also back there,
never to find some parts, I carried
before, in my first steps from home.

Once I could join friends at a bar,
in the movies or in the stands,
without having to sit uneasily
with my back to the wall.
Once I could sleep without that
hunting knife under my pillow.
Once I didn't jump at backfires,
gunfire, fireworks, wind-slammed
doors and creaking floors,
balloons popping at Woolworths stores,
that left me butt riding the escalator,
down to the ice cream bar.

Once I didn't resent so many people,

looking down their noses so they
would not see us, from that 'damn war.'
Resent the Legion barkeep who said
they were too full for new guys,
the drunk at the end of the bar
spoke up, as that dude walked away,
you guys are just not the right stuff
anymore, like the wars before.
Once I drove with caution,
not like I was bullet proof,
Once no one whispered
baby killer, he's a baby killer,
as I walked to the line
in the college cafeteria,
but said it so low, that it could
have been anybody, anyone.
Once I did not know
the depth of anger and rage.

Once I thought my family
would want to know:
about me and the war,
about me in the war,
how I had felt more alive,
about my burden of memories.
I thought they would ask,
but they didn't.

Their Names by Dorian Dula

His name was Terry Boyce. He was from East St. Louis, Illinois. Not exactly a garden spot of a city. Terry came to Charlie 1/5 (1st Battalion, 5th Marine Regiment) in the Fall of 1967. We were located in the Que Son Valley which was home to the NVA's 2nd Division. I think Terry had just gotten in country when Operation Swift happened in early September, 1967. Terry was attached to my squad.

Delta Company was in a Defensive Perimeter near Dong Son just off our Hill. On September 4th Delta. Co. was attacked and overrun by the 2nd NVA Division. Bravo Co. was sent to help out. Alpha and Charlie Co. were in other locations doing sweeps and platoon-sized patrols.

Eventually Alpha and Charlie entered the fray. It was Terry's first firefight. Units from the 2nd and 3rd Marine Battalion came to help. Operation Swift concluded on 15 September, in which 127 Marines and Corpsman died.

Welcome to Vietnam, Terry.

In late January, the Tet Offensive of 1968 was launched by the enemy. The Imperial City of Hue was overrun by enemy forces. Somewhere between 3,000-5,000 civilians were slaughtered and buried in mass graves prior to American forces making it to the city.

In early February, the 2nd or 3rd, we were told to saddle up. We could tell by the intensity and inflection in the Company Commander's voice that something big was happening, but we didn't know what. We loaded onto 6 trucks and headed to the river where we then were loaded onto boats and headed into Hue. Pulling into Hue, we could see from our river boat lights and some cameras. As we got closer we could tell it was Walter Cronkite talking with some Marine officers. We all looked at each other and knew we were into something big. We unloaded and were given instructions on what to do. We split up into platoons and squads and began sweeping through the city. There was not much resistance for the first few days but some occasional sniper fire. But my squad didn't receive any casualties from these skirmishes. We had a machine gun team attached to my squad. So there were twelve or thirteen men, I can't remember. We stopped at a house on the early evening of 17 February and set up watch for the night. My shift was the last one, just before dawn. But before my shift, we were awakened by gunfire hitting our house. It was coming from a school adjacent to the house occupied by our own men. We got on the radio with them and asked them what the hell was going on. They told us our house was surrounded by "gooks," which as most of you know is a derogatory name for the enemy.

I went into an adjacent room where we heard some noise and I emptied my whole magazine as I sprayed the room. As I was about to load my next magazine, in the doorway was a gook. I hadn't slammed the magazine home yet and he had the drop on me and I thought I was dead. He turned and ran away. Then I yelled, "A gook, a gook, a f'ing gook!" McKnight pulled the pin on a grenade and threw it into the room.

I don't know what happened, but the grenade came back into our room where most of us were. I don't know if they threw it back or it hit something and bounced back. I saw it come back and yelled, "It came back." Boyce and I were near the door to the courtyard between the houses. Boyce ran out first and I was right behind him. They opened up on us and we were both hit. Terry died instantly. I got my bullet in my upper right thigh. It went all the way through. I hopped back into the house as they were still firing at me. The grenade went off and several men were wounded with the shrapnel. Some seriously.

Terry's girlfriend didn't wait for him and was then going to marry some other guy. Terry's only hope was to make it home to go to the wedding because he just wanted her to be happy. He's a better man than I would be.

Terry's name is on the wall on Panel 40E, line 1.

Roy Vernon Berry was from Tracy, CA.

Not far from where I grew up in Visalia, CA. We were both Central California boys. Farm Country. I think Berry got to Vietnam in May 1967, a month after I did. We hit it off right away. We patrolled the Que Son Valley for the balance of that summer, culminating in September on Operation Swift as I previously mentioned. Later that Fall we moved to

Phu Loc south of Phu Bai where the 3rd Marine Division HQ are. We were in a valley surrounded by mountains on three sides and the Pacific Ocean on the other side.

I'm not sure what military genius put us in that valley but the NVA and VC dropped mortars in on us day and night. We dug trenches and extra bunkers for as much safety as we could. One night the mortars were coming in on us. They were walking them in closer and closer. Berry and I were in a trench, huddled together. Berry was shaking like a leaf. This big, 6'3" 235 pound football player was scared to death, as we all were.

When we got to Hue, Berry had his own squad and they were sweeping next to us. Before we were attacked that morning on the 18th, we saw Berry wounded and crawling in the courtyard. Not sure why he was in the courtyard by himself. Boyce and I said we got to go get him. Boyce said, "You've been over here longer than I have, I'm going." Just then, an automatic weapon burst ended Berry's life.

Roy Vernon Berry is located on the Wall at Panel 39E, Line 79.

Michael Warren was from Golden, Colorado.

Mike was the one of the few in my squad that I didn't have much personal interaction with. He was a quiet kid. He wore glasses and looked kind of studious. He did his job and did what I told him to about positioning, etc.

When the grenade went off, Mike took the worst of it. He was in a lot of pain and we tried to comfort him as much as we could, except we were all wounded, including the corpsman. We comforted him and told him it was going to be all right. It took an hour before reinforcements got to us and got us out. Mike suffered the whole time and we could tell he was in extreme pain. Mike Warren died the next day on February 19th.

Michael Warren's name is on Panel 40E, Line 34.

All 3 of these brave Marines were 19 years old. Rest in Peace, heroes.

Special at the NC Playhouse (4/17/22) by Rob Kuebler

He brings out good feelings in most all people
Heads the pack with positive thoughts to the top of the steeple
Singing Neil Diamond hits was CherryCherry Band
They took to Scott like a magic wand
Gave him a well-worn Native Veteran Marine hat
Took his picture up front with Steve and that
Was just the beginning with shirt, beads and placard
What a big day for someone dealt the death card
He just is not ready and a couple of months late
God, apparently decided to adjust the date
He slowly declines but has a great attitude
And does not like to wait for his meal food
"Strong Eagle" enjoyed the music and attention
Steve and the band need honorable mention.

The Letter Never Sent by John Sitman

I paused before walking across the tarmac
to get on that freedom bird home.
I had long waited to get to this point.
I thought of the days I had doubts.
When you're young, death seems a foreign word, until you go to war.
Then, it becomes a discerning sword.
Flying into an LZ to pick up wounded had its own strain
but flying in to pick up soldiers gone was a whole different ball game.
With wounded there was hope.
With the dead only agony and pain.

The pilot was trained to fly the Huey.
The soldier on the ground was trained to kill the enemy.
The Doctors, nurses and medics were trained to help the wounded.
But, no one was trained for the pain and sorrow, the trauma, the
screaming,
the bleeding, and the mess it made when you cleaned off the deck of the
Huey.
And no training prepares you for being asked point blank,
"Am I going to die?" As if I knew or had magic of some kind.
You tell him, you tell yourself, "You are going to be alright,"
but you know, it's just a blind lie?
You give your best confident face, but what you said felt like a disgrace.
I only did that twice; it became too much to embrace.
There's that part of you shaken and wrenching inside
because you lied to ease that dying soldier's mind;
but there was no time for that.
You had a job to do, you had to stay focused.
There was always more to do.
It was never routine,
especially when a soldier died while I held his head on my knees.
How does a young soldier try and deal with that?

So, I prepared a letter, in case something went wrong.
I felt I had cheated death, especially since my friends were gone.
Why am I still here? Why am I still able to breath?
That was the feeling that got me more than the rest,
so I tried not to think of it and bury it like the rest.
One day after landing, I noticed a shell had ripped through my vest.
It wasn't the first-time death tried to deliver,
there were other times shells slid by and missing me by a sliver.

I decided to write a letter to my folks
to express my deepest heartfelt love.
I did not expect to see them again
because life around me seemed not to hold.

So, I began the letter with:
If you have received this letter, then I have passed.
I love you so much. A son couldn't have asked for better folks.
I'm sorry for anything I have done to cause you hurt or pain,
but I want you to know this most:
I love you more than I can say.
Please remember me the way I was,
the man you have made,
the man I have become:
a soldier that did his duty without hesitation or complaint.
I was hoping to come home like my brothers
but, I'm sorry, Mom, I won't be coming home like them.
Thank you for letting me be what I thought I should be.
Thank you for believing in me with your great love;
and, Dad, thank you for being the tough example of a man so strong.
My eternal love always, your son John.

I kept this letter nearly two months in my front fatigue pocket.
I told my pilot about it, so he knew where it was if my time came.
I had to write the letter over once. It had gotten too wet

because I carried it everywhere, I went.

When the time came for me to get on that freedom bird home,

I stopped short of the plane,

my best intention no longer needed.

I took the letter from my pocket and looked at it with relief

this letter that held the sad surprise filled with such grief.

I tore up the letter, knowing it would have been the last I would have sent.

I never told my folks of the letter I had ready to be sent,

because I was able to do what I was hoping to do,

and that was to take myself instead.

I was one step closer to being on my way home,

relieved that that letter never made it out of Vietnam.

I Used to Be by Frank Cucumber

I used to be easygoing, with not a care in the world around me.
It was me in a world of my own.
Young, with a lot to learn.
After high school, I studied auto mechanics in trade school for a year.
After that, I worked for the Bureau of Indian Affairs in the Department of the Interior.
Then a change happened to me. I was drafted but joined the Army – there I was made over.
The Drill Instructor at Fort Gordon, Georgia made me who I am now.
A mind lost forever.
Just a new skill and angry.
I made a living working as a mason.
After Vietnam, working indoors was not for me.
I made a living for my family, but I was angry at the world and didn't know why.
But I now understand PTSD.

Sitting by David Robinson

As I sit and wonder, as I sit and grow old
As I think of for whom the bells toll
Or for whom does the bugle blow

How many millions have fought and died,
Fighting for every side
How many bugles have blown
As we have buried our own
How many wives, children, mom and dad,
Brothers and sisters, friends and comrades
Have wept and cried and been so sad
Oh, how can we ever forget the bad?

As I sit and ponder
And think of the things that happened back yonder
Then I wonder why wasn't it me
Oh, how many times I'd like to flee
But then I remember, oh, can't you see
That all these died that we might be free.

Memorial Day and Everyday Heroes by Ron Toler

To me, Memorial Day is a day not only to honor those that made the ultimate sacrifice in the service of this great land, but also a time to recognize those everyday heroes who returned from war and went on to do their part to build this land of freedom.

It is a time to honor those who served in the trenches of Europe, surviving the bullets, the mustard gas, and the barbed wire to free the continent from oppression.

It is a time to honor those of the Greatest Generation who served all over the world. It's time to honor Grady, who left his beloved Betty to fly his B-17 in support of the invasion of Normandy. It's time to honor the quiet Uncle Rip who felt the burden of living a good life to honor so many of his fallen brothers as they stormed the beaches of Normandy.

It is a time to honor those who fought in Korea, many who had survived WWII, and Uncle Bill Sitman who made the ultimate sacrifice to save his 5-man squad. To honor Dick Overstreet who lost his life flying his F-84E on a bombing run against a train south of Pan Man Jung.

It's a time to honor the Baby Boomers for the service in Vietnam. The Davids and Lesters who were called Doc, who struggled to save their wounded brothers. Time to honor the Blakeslys and Johns who flew their helicopter in harm's way to bring those wounded to safety and medical help. It's time to honor the Allans who had to make the hard decisions and worked compassionately to save and heal those in their care.

It is a time to honor a country boy who returned from war, put his head down and went to work, only to sum up his generation's experience of turbulent times in a beautiful poem, "Brothers and Sisters Like These."

It's time to honor the Bills who, after serving as a Marine in the jungles of Vietnam finished his career as a Gunny, leading his troops to build airfields in the far north of Desert Storm. It's time to honor the Altons who, after flying his Super Saber and Sandy in Vietnam, led his squadron over downtown Baghdad in their stealthy 117's.

It's time to honor the Tommys and Stacies and Kevins, who left the safety and security of home to serve in the deserts of Iraq in an all-volunteer force, enduring the heat, separation and hardship to make the world a better place.

It's also time to honor the Dr. K's, the Josephs, the Elizabeths, Jeremiahs, Jeffs and Marybeths, who recognized the trauma those returning heroes suffered and worked tirelessly to help relieve their stress.

It is time to recognize your neighbors, the mothers and fathers who lost their children in service to this great land. The Ann and Dale Hamptons who lost their only daughter, Kimberly, in Iraq. It's time to honor Ann, who told us of the loss of her son Matthew from a loving mother's perspective.

Memorial Day is a time to remember and honor all those patriots, present and past, who sacrificed their lives while serving this great country in helping make the world a better, freer place. It is a time to honor those who returned home and have since died from their war-related illnesses and diseases. They are not to be forgotten.

The Tower by Midge Lorence

This tower isn't made of steel like the one in France, or with Masonary like the one in Italy. But, it took a hell of a lot of blood, sweat, and tears to keep the son of a gun standing.

It was a tower that could be your best friend or worst nightmare. At times during the day it could be almost peaceful. A warm breeze would usher in the pungent smell of last night's brief but deadly fire fight. I couldn't help but think it, as satan's cologne!

It could be a quiet place to write home and for your mind to wander. One time I saw a perfect white cross in a deep blue sky and I wondered if that cross could be seen back home, minus the sounds and smells of war.

Some of us called the tower the last church of separation between good and evil. We called it a church because three Chaplains of different faiths at different times left three things. The priest left Rosery beads, the Protestant minister prayers from the King James Bible, and the Rabbi left the Star of David. It was comforting to look up and see the symbols of faith. They were placed on a header support beam and no swearing or pornography were allowed on that side of the tower.

As long as we weren't in the shit, night could be a symphony of sounds and a magical show of lights seen and heard from our balcony seats 30 feet above the contaminated soil below us. Who the hell am I kidding?

Between the concertina wire and the bush was a strip of nothing, a 150 to 300 foot wide strip of land we called the agent orange beach of death. ARVN Soldiers would respray the beach monthly from the back of a deuce and a half. The crazy bastards were soaked in it.

To me the time I spent on duty in that tower and what happened there are things I try to forget but also things that I try to remember. If I could describe the tower in one word it would be time.

At times it seemed so damn boring that time seemed to stand still. Other times when the shit hit the fan it flew by almost as fast as the AK rounds that were coming back at us.

Loading Rounds by Michael White

I push the magazine release,
hear the familiar sound
of metal sliding on metal,
it falls to my left hand.

With my right hand,
I position the first round
between my thumb and index finger.
It could be the round
of broken relationships
not the first but
one of many,
they didn't ask,
why was I so wrong?
Nor did I know what to say,
lost in my ignorance.

A second round, this one
is hot much like my temper.

The third round slides in too easily,
self-medication could last a lifetime.

The next, hard to load
needing multiple tries
to get clean,
through many inpatient stays.

This round was hard to see,
much like myself,
for years the one that cared

never knew where I was.

Next round was expensive,
much like all my lawless deeds
that I paid for with lost respect.

This round was wet,
just like all the tears we shed,

This round is red,
I suppose for the 53 dead
who did not come home.

One after another,
I pack them in the magazine

The next one getting tighter?
Leave a round missing,
the void in my life.
For the next ten years
I would shoot/reload these rounds.

Oh God the people I've hurt,
till finally one day there's no more
rounds or people in my sights.

Until I found a power
greater than myself,
with his hand on mine,
I found my way
one day at a time,
not to hurt myself or others,
oh God, forgive me
for what have I done.

Silence by Gerry Nieters

I never thought I could turn off my emotions. In Vietnam I did. We all did. I couldn't allow my emotions to cloud my judgment. I couldn't allow the horrors of war to find open emotional expression. After a while, my emotional expressions were nonexistent. My affect was flat. In essence, I didn't feel. Life was a robotic behavior of just doing my job. I simply existed. I simply performed.

Now I find those emotions weren't turned off at all. They were submerged, smoldering in my subconscious, always there, always under lock and key. But they are like a volcano, held back by the thin crust over the boiling cauldron.

Keep the inferno covered, lest it erupt and blast me into a place of stored horrors that I am afraid to go.

Amazing Grace by Jim Hugenschmidt

Is there such a thing as a just war? Yes, if we are defending ourselves, or if we are defending others from aggression. So, what was our justification for going to war in Vietnam?

In 1954 the Vietnamese drove out the French. By the terms of the Geneva Accords, the country was temporarily administratively divided at the 17th parallel, with elections to be held by July 1956 to create a reunified Vietnamese state. And elections are the American way—in our Declaration of Independence we say that "Governments are instituted among Men, deriving their just powers by the consent of the governed."

Ho Chi Minh was the revolutionary hero in driving out the French. He was Vietnam's George Washington. Our intelligence corps estimated that in an election Ho would win the Presidency by a wide margin. But Ho was a Communist, and we didn't want Vietnam becoming a domino falling to Communism. Instead of letting the Vietnamese people decide democratically, our government exerted pressure. The election never happened. Predictably, war happened.

When we ignominiously left Vietnam in 1975, Ho Chi Minh became president. Vietnam assumed its place in the family of nations. It has been peaceful and has prospered. Exactly what was it we were saving Vietnam from?

On the Vietnam Memorial Wall we rightly honor the 58,220 American soldiers who gave their lives. We mourn them and commemorate their sacrifice. But we as a country fail to reckon other sacrifices, other losses.

We have done far too little for the families of those who died, and for the veterans who suffered physical disability or PTSD. And all who served in the war are forever changed. Many suicides, broken marriages, addictions, bankruptcies, and other misfortunes may be traced to the immense difficulty of reconciling the brutality of war with the natural humanity of our souls and the goodness we were brought up to cherish. We should take better care of those who served us.

But our focus is largely limited to what happened to us. Compare our 58,220 dead to the estimates of the Vietnamese killed, ranging from a low of 1,150,000 to a high of 3,194,000, many of them children, women, elderly, and other non-combatants. These are just the dead. Not the disabled. Not those suffering PTSD. Not the widows and orphans and broken families. Not the property destruction. Not the Agent Orange and other environmental consequences. Not the unexploded ordnance. Not the lasting horror of children growing up in a war. We have done nothing in recompense. As a country, we do not acknowledge the harm we caused.

War is an atrocity that makes atrocities. On March 16, 1968, at My Lai, as many as 504 non-combatants were massacred. They included women, children, infants, and the elderly. Warrant Officer Hugh Thompson, Jr. was piloting a helicopter in support of our troops. From the air, he saw what was happening; he landed and intervened. He is credited with stopping the slaughter.

On the 50th anniversary of My Lai, Thompson returned there. He met people who had survived that day. One woman, who had been a teenager at the time and found a place to hide, asked him, "Why have the others not returned, so that we can forgive them?" Her desire to forgive those who had slaughtered her family and others in her village, who had subjected this young girl to such horror and terror, is an act of grace, amazing in the circumstances.

Having served honorably does not absolve us of our burden of having participated in an unjust war. We can heal only by knowing our history, confronting it honestly. Then we must give back as we can to help those in need, whomever and wherever. And we must consciously forgive—others, our country, and finally ourselves.

Grace need not be amazing; it can be how we live. It can be our salvation.

Legacy of Who Am I by Allan Perkal

I am a 75-year-old Philly Boy, entering the fourth quarter of my life, who lives in the mountains of western North Carolina—who would have thought that!

I am a member of a tribe called Brothers and Sisters Like These

I am dedicated to the mission of making a difference in the lives of those who served their country in war.

I am first generation US Citizen of Polish parents who came to this country to find freedom from persecution.

I am a medic who served in the Vietnam War that defined what his life was to be!

I am a loving husband and grandfather who has been blessed being part of their lives.

I am a human being who believes in a cause greater than myself.

I am a passionate person who will meet his maker knowing I did my best to make a difference in this world.

The Day Before I Left by Dean Little

There were two parts of me the last day before I left. The outside part was busy stuffing my uniforms, boots and travel papers into my duffle bag. Too, I was tying up loose ends with friends and family. My mother would stop at the bedroom door for the umpteenth time to ask if she could help in any way. Her facial expression was constricted at times, and sometimes I could hear a tremor in her voice. But like on the day I left for boot camp, she would not cry, which would have been a relief for her but might make me feel bad. That is the way she was. My younger sisters had already given me sealed letters, filled with little girl ideas of war and leaving. I was to open them when I needed to remember they loved me. My grandparents had said goodbye the day before at their cottage on the lake, as had my three brothers, all married and living across town. My Dad had taken me out for drinks, reminiscences, jokes, and laughter the night before. I was still a little hungover as flight time approached. My father had divorced my mom, breaking her heart, the year before, so I was not going to see both at the airport.

The inner part of me had been busy memorizing the tree in our front yard, my bedroom with boxes of books under the bed, in the closet, my baseball, bowling, other trophies on the dresser. I ruminated on my personal insistence that I needed to serve my country, how I had volunteered for the US Army, volunteered for combat medic training and three times volunteered for Vietnam service while at my last duty station. Would I regret my decisions, would I live up to the demands of being in a war zone? Continually I wondered, would I live to return home to my family, return to college, return whole in mind and body, and move on into my future life?

In the mid-day my flights took me to Travis Air Force Base in northern California. There we were herded, given shots, processed, and moved into giant repurposed airplane hangars, filled with seemingly endless rows of bunks, and also row upon row of telephone booths for last calls home. Our food came from batteries of machines rotating out sandwiches, cups of soup, desserts, and sodas. Before they locked the doors that night to keep some from going AWOL, I made my way to a small, attached library. I hand copied The Unbeliever's Prayer from John Gunther's *Death Be Not Proud* and carried it with me in Vietnam.

Work details were completed, and the daylight waned. After several calls to my siblings and mom, I called my father last. He quickly reminded me that midnight on the west coast was three am in Syracuse, but then said he was glad I had called. Our relationship had grown emotionally distanced since the divorce. I did not enjoy this estrangement especially since I might never see him again. He was a big, rugged guy, a Steamfitter by trade, a platoon sergeant in WWII, a coach of many kids' baseball and basketball teams. He was the Arm-Wrestling champion of North Syracuse in his thirties, he was smart and a crooner in his outside part. Some need, trauma, pain in his inside part, probably PTSD from WWII, led him to drink too much. Drinking could release his dark anger. Our angry dad was frightening and at times he would batter his wife and his children. All of us were drawn to his dynamic charisma and recurrently repelled and saddened by his violence. I called my dad last, not sure if I could tell him that I loved him. When he had answered the call, he wanted to know "how it was going." I gave him the low down about the lock down. He said that troops were locked into cattle cars when moved up to the front lines in WWII. I kept ending every other sentence with "and one more thing" meaning to say those words declaring emotional attachment despite injuries to my mom in particular and to my outside and inside self.

Finally, I got out "And one more thing Dad, ... I love you." There was a breathy exhalation on the line. At first, I thought, with dismay, that he was laughing at my statement. Then the sounds clarified to become soft sobbing. His voice became huskier with emotion. When he could vocalize, he replied, "I love you too son, be safe. Please come home."

Filled with my own emotions, elation, hopefulness, and sadness too, I was ready to go.

Redeployment: 2008 by Stacie Listenberger

The word that is always discussed for the entire deployment.
The plans for re-de
money saved: buy a new car
            or a motorcycle
new baby- squeeze the new one
new love- make new promises
new friends and old- let's drink and get over the war.

All the thoughts and more
glitter and move around in all of us
    as we prepare to re-de and go back home

in the hours before our plane's wheels leave the tarmac

in the hours before we all scream and cheer
in unified glee to know the sand will now be far way

we are still a hardened clan of Soldiers --

we still have time to tell a tale for two
in ways that are never told once back on peaceful lands.
This story starts and ends with shouts of "no brass, no ammo"
 a full out scream we learn in basic training along with kill, kill, ice cold
steal.

In this tent in the last 6 to 8 hours of our combat time

we empty our two duffle bags (yes you know the ones)
into wooded squares that are waist high
to ensure we don't have any live ammo or spent brass.

In ways demoralizing
like trust me- I signed up
and that we all spend days, hours and for some minutes packing these
bags

I know my hands had scrapes on them
from so tightly pushing everything into
any give in my bag

No brass- no ammo I loudly shout
this releases tension of going home
how do we cross that line?

The NCO comes by and checks my gear.
Loud tap, I am good, repack
shout again- no brass, no ammo.

As I walk with all pockets cleaned
I walk through a chute of metal detectors
again- no brass, no ammo

I set out to the big white tents
filled with pre-packaged food and water
a large screen TV on the other end

Four or more hours to go- sit back and just dream
I was a Major, rank clear on my collar
because of my rank - no one was to sit around me

a young Marine- so young you would have guessed 16
smiles broadly and sits beside me
-- almost snuggling in

I am sure I made a noise, a warning of some kind to let him know
Yet, I quickly realize - he was young and had a secret to tell

And story he started to tell
once he started my Major rank fell
    and I would never tell.

In that tent- Soldiers sprawled everywhere
he dug deep into his boot and pulled out a spent 5-50 round

He got it past no brass - no ammo

The brass was his marker
of being alive during his combat time

This Ammo when fully ready to discharge from his weapon
Jammed during a firefight
this young gunner saving his men- fixed the ammo jam
-- as the smoke cleared a bit
-- he had a moment to see
as his weapon was cleared back to kill

The war Marines realized in emotion
as the young and still innocent do
had his weapon fired
he would have killed children
the innocent not far from him

We just sat together

A Major and a Marine
Emotion not spoken out loud
yet, clearly shared

During an honest moment
Thank God, he did not have to live
with the thought of killing children

before we re-deploy
carry on
please carry on

No brass, No ammo

My First Six Days in the Bush by Steve Henderson

After I arrived in Vietnam I was sent to Quang-tri to meet up with India Company ¾ 3rd Marine Division. I was issued all my gear and went thru a makeshift orientation that proved not to prepare me for anything. I was flown by CH53 helicopter to the Vandegrift combat base nicknamed STUD, where I met up with my company.

There we stood in lines for 24-hours before heading to the bush.

I was taken by chopper to the DMZ to hump patrols for the next three weeks. The first day in the bush was somewhat uneventful, dealing with the heat and leeches, and the weight of the gear was enough. Second day in the bush after two hours of humping we got into a firefight with the NVA. This is when I realized what all my training had been about. When I was told to move out amidst the fire around us, I moved out and did my job. After the firefight was over, we did our first body count…we had killed several NVAs. This touched me in a surreal way, but I noticed the Marines that had been there for months, this was just a regular day of work for them.

The third day in the bush, this young man I had met, he was the largest man in the platoon, a six-foot-four-inch Polish kid from New England. I remember he had a great smile. The gunnery sergeant informed him that morning that he would be walking point that day. After being in a firefight the previous day, everyone was somewhat on edge and alert. Several hours into the patrol that day, a shot rang out from an AK47 I assumed to be a sniper. The bullet hit this good looking Marine and we watched the navy corpsman work on him until he succumbed to his wounds. It was like a horrible nightmare unfolding before me. The radio man called in for a medi-vac …two choppers flew in over us and radioed back they were unable to land due to large concentrations of NVAs on three sides of us. They said they would try again the following day.

Day 4 we all took turns carrying this Marine in a body bag…trying not to fathom what we were really doing. We had to keep moving due to concentration of the enemy and get away from the horseshoe of the

NVA around us. The chopper could not land safely on the 4th day. Needless to say, carrying this Marine around was taking a toll on all of us both physically and mentally.

On the 5th day we continued to hump to a safer place, taking turns with the body bag. On the 6th day we were out of sea rations, water and ammo due to the firefight we had earlier. Radio contact confirmed helicopters were returning to get the body and bring us needed supplies. The chopper dropped our supplies first, and then we hoisted out the body bag and one injured man due to heat exhaustion.

The first six days in the bush I felt I became a grown man. This time made me realize that I would do whatever it took to get my fellow Marines and myself out of the bush alive each day. I have always wondered how this affected this man's family and friends….and why he was denied the life he could of had.

Right Place, Right Time by Ron Kuebler

As my comrade dug under me to avoid rockets and bombs
I thought how lucky I am to be in the calms
Those times I thought I was dead for sure
Keeping my cool seemed to be the cure
But luck is a big item to count
Survival is definitely out of a fount
That no one understands but pays fealty to
And thanks constantly for life which may be due
A few of us are so lucky to survive just fine
I missed a recon flight by answering the call of nature
So many killed on that flight but I was not mature
Enough to hustle on board or grab a strut
So they said "there he is, what a nut"
Can't join us know you are too late
Maybe we will just be their bait
To take the rounds, but not you mate.

To the CAV by David Rozelle

In February the Big Red One packed its duffel bag and went home. I was left in the war zone and shuffled off to a replacement company in Bien Hoa. During the four days I waited there for assignment to a new company, the rumor and wisdom floating around the compound was "anywhere is fine as long as you don't go to the 1st Cav. Man, they are getting half a company wiped out every day." The relocation papers I finally got started with "to C Company 15th Medical Battalion, 1st Calvary."

Brimming with confidence, I flew into the dust-soaked airstrip of the one-time French rubber tree plantation near the Cambodian Border then called Quan Loi. Still looking for good omens and positive thoughts, I pitched my duffel bag on the back of the jeep/ambulance my new company had sent to fetch me. As I was stretching my leg into the passenger seat, a Chinook Helicopter like the one I had arrived at the airfield in, screamed over my head. This one was fixed with a cargo net every bit as large as the chopper itself. Something did not look just right about the plane. Half into the jeep I watched, dumbstruck, as the big, overgrown banana-looking ship jumped upward as much as forward into the cloudless sky and broke savagely into two equal pieces no more than 200 yards outside the security fence of the base camp and left six crew members dead in its wake.

I got to the new company area before all the excitement of the recovery of casualties from the helicopter had run its course, but I was aware only of the high activity. When I reported to the company headquarters I did find one bit of positive news. The company clerk was a fellow I had been close to during medic training in Texas. He was alone in the office and gave me a quick lesson on the day to day working of the company. In its infinite wisdom the U.S. Army sent a set number of men to each such medical company. This number was set in Washington, DC, and the men who went to the medical companies were trained in Texas and given the job skill I.D. number of medical aid men. That number was

91 A or some advanced variety of it. The medical company needed people to do things other than treat the wounded. They had a motor pool, cooks, clerical staff, radio operators, supervisors and ward medics at a minimum. All these other jobs had army job I.D. numbers, but in the case of the army medical companies in Vietnam, the company was allowed to assign jobs to the men who showed up on their door step according to "the needs of the army."

In the company I had been shipped to the responsibility of sorting all this out was held by the company clerk, my buddy. To show off his power, this clerk, my friend, asked me what job I wanted in the company, and just like I had good sense, I quickly said, "I want to do surgery and medical stuff." Then just as quickly this clerk made a few marks on an official looking piece of paper and I was placed. He then asked me if I had a driver's license. I had no idea the army even issued driver's licenses and told him so. He pulled a pad of forms from a drawer in his neat as a pin desk, wrote a few words and handed me the document. Seems part of the job included driving the jeep/ambulance and now I was legal.

With the important aspects of my new home and assignment complete, my friend and clerk personally took me to my sleeping bunker, showed me the shower and latrine and accompanied me to the mess hall where the afternoon meal was in progress.

Once the eating was polished off, I was escorted to the facility which was to be my work duty assignment. The physicians and high-level medical staff had completed the routine work for the day when we finally got to the treatment bunker. The Company Commander was standing in the shade bunker, holding court with an enlisted man concerning the Japanese political culture prior to WWII, or that was as near to the meat of the conference as I understood it. My clerk waited for a break in the conversation and introduced me to him. The CO was a tall, thin, and unsubstantial person from Kansas. His hair had the wave, color and consistency of corn silk a week before harvest. He wore a clean uniform with the appropriate officer insignia, but his bearing was less military and more cloistered nun. There was nothing about him that suggested he would be able to administer an antibiotic shot for fear it might cause the patient undue pain. Knee-deep in a profession dedicated and proud of its down and dirty image, this man was so clean it hurt. I took an instant like to the man.

We had talked a very few minutes when a mud-caked jeep charged up to us. There was a lifeless body of an equally mud-caked soldier slumped in the passenger seat of the jeep. My clerk friend and the clean-shirted man talking with the CO suddenly remembered important business they just had to attend. They bolted. The CO quickly found a litter and we took the wounded into the treatment room. The commander doctor took a quick look and asked me if I had ever performed a chest tube procedure. My blank look was answer enough. He briefly explained that the man bleeding in his chest cavity had collapsed his lung. The surgical procedure was simply to cut a small hole in the chest cavity and insert a medical grade water hose into the chest cavity to empty the blood and let the lung re-inflate. Emboldened with ignorance, I agreed to perform it. The CO looked at me and said simply, "I'll talk you through it."

The necessary tools appeared from somewhere and calling out what little sterile technique I had been exposed to, I started. For no logical reason I thought this was just what every lowly combat medic did when they were moved out of field duty. With no break in the job since the Jeep arrived, I found myself cutting a three-inch hole in the man's rib cage where my doctor had indicated with the intention of inserting the tube my new doctor friend was holding.

Once the skin was breached I was told to take the pair of blunt scissors handed me and I aggressively worked them into the white under the skin. At this point things failed to go according to plan. When I entered the chest cavity, I was greeted with more blood than I had seen total in my life. It was warm, dark red with occasional pockets of bubbles and bright red, and sticky all over. I was so surprised or unprepared for the outcome that I stood frozen while my legs and feet were soaked and recolored by the discharge. The operation stopped at this point and became a teaching opportunity. The young soldier had been beyond repair and the operation I performed was more of a test to see if I had the nervous system to do this work all day every day. For a second or two the motor pool assignment looked inviting.

Before I had too much time to reconsider, I was informed gently that "no military job is complete until all the paperwork is in order." I was introduced to the DD forms from Graves Registration which declares to the immediate world that another good man is no longer with us. The service man's serial number satisfies all the major questions. The matter of cause of death and signature of attending physician affixed to the army paperwork closes the book, chapter and verse, of a promising life.

I initialed and attached the TD tag that follows the remains of our dead friends. Then I helped the doctor gently lift the mortal remains in a black plastic-coated bag and zip the bag securely. The doctor and I then carried the package to the twelve by twelve outbuilding, which served as the company morgue, completing a process with which I was to become much too familiar.

Hawkeye by Gerry Nieters

As a physician, my burden was not a physical one. It was mental. The army provided me with the tools of healing, just as the infantryman was furnished with the tools of killing. Mine wasn't the shoulder straining back crushing weight of a field pack. It was the emotional weight of doing the best for the men under my care.

Hospital duty was little different than stateside hospital work. There was no real danger. We weren't issued weapons. But like many infantrymen, we were mainly draftees. We didn't want to be there. Although physical hardships were few, there was the universal yearning for home, family, and friends.

I had just finished my internship training, was drafted, and sent to Vietnam. This would be my first experience outside of the ivory towers. The dichotomy of emotions took some time to permeate my psyche. I wasn't treating medical illnesses that one unintentionally contracted. I was treating wounds intentionally inflicted on another person. Man's inhumanity to man. And why were we all there in the first place? We were never given a realistic reason. Anyway, that was my job. That was my training. But what did that ultimately lead to? It led to discharging the men back into the savage meatgrinder of battle. Maybe they wouldn't be so lucky the next time. So, what was I really doing?

The ambivalence of emotions led to a love/hate emotional relationship within myself. I loved the fact that I could restore them to health. I hated the fact that I had to put them in harm's way once again. The dichotomy of emotions increased with each dreaded discharge.

I never talked to my fellow physicians about my feelings. Perhaps it was egotism. Perhaps it was thinking there was mental weakness on my part. I was supposed to be a healer, not in need of healing myself. I looked forward to the alcohol at the end of the day.

I now not only understand but feel the subtle underlying theme of M.A.S.H. 4077.

Untitled by James Watts

Being in Northern Corp it was not unusual for combat controls to visit Quang Tri, a click north, and enter the DMZ, better known as the Demilitarized Zone. On this day fourteen Marines—ten Riflemen, one Machine Gunner, one M79 Grenade man, one Radioman and one Corpsman—left our base and headed towards the Rock Pile.

Our platoon made these trips numerous times in the past, but a soldier's instinct told me this was not going to be a patrol that ended well. Four hours into the patrol through mountainous terrain, we underwent sniper fire, which soon became small arms fire from the southwest flank. One soldier was wounded, not too serious. We found ourselves pinned until we could map out where all the Vietcong fire power was coming from. Didn't take long. We soon set up a perimeter in the thick jungle and continued to hold our ground. This went on for four long hours, with two more being wounded. One soldier was hit in the shoulder, and the other in the leg. Our M79 Machine Gunner, and several Riflemen finished the VC off. With no landing zone to help with the wounded, we resumed our patrol towards Camp Carrol (RP).

I helped a fellow Marine, by the name of George, who was shot in the leg, step by step through the treacherous terrain of the Vietnam jungle. One arm around my neck, he used his M-16 as a crutch with the other. It was definitely an eye-opening experience for a lot of us! I had only been in the country a mere three weeks, and some others, less.

What I Carried Inside by Michael White

I really tried not to focus too much on these things,
yet it was a small voice in my darkened heart.
It's what made the family wide-eyed, and they teared with joy.
I heard others whisper words of gratitude to Him
when I shared too many close-call accounts
of death brushing past me.
Why was it them and not I?
Was it the secret briefing by a man from Texas, which lasted two days,
that warned of and described the "evil doers?"

Maybe it was the conditioning to move our eyes in such a way, mimicking that old wall clock cat with a moving tail as well. It was definitely some of the foreign jargon we learned to yell back to the post when things got dicey, sure it was. The countless taxpayers' dollars paid off some. Especially the dollars for the cold steel that we slung around our shoulders that loved to chew brass and spit lead.

But those other times, times when things didn't add up and we didn't really talk about it. When we were looking at the aftermath in silence but having the loudest conversation with our eyes and head slightly cocked in disbelief.

One group calls it a "Higher Power," others God, still others call it fate. Whatever you want to call it, it's the reason we are here today. The reason I'm able to read this to you. It is something bigger than all of us, something that I've carried in my heart for a long time.

Magic T-Shirt by Tommy Cannon

As I remember three years of war, I most often think of the bad times. The truth is that there are more good times than bad. You always miss your family and your home, but you will have moments that are there to remember and put a smile on your face. Playing spades with the guys, or Pete trying to ride the donkey, David teaching me how to play cribbage, and we played almost every day. After hearing stories from the Brothers and Sisters, it started to let my mind go to those places and remember some amazing moments from Iraq.

During my time in Mosul there were a lot of bad things I could tell you about, but I would like to tell you about a couple wonderful things that happened.

There was a young man we would pass almost every day who was obviously mentally handicapped. To the people there, this young man would not produce children or add to their wealth so he was not taken care of. He played with a plastic bottle and would wave to us every time he saw us. We waved back, and when we were on foot, we would give him food and water. One day as we passed, one of my Soldiers saw that his tongue was stuck in the bottle. As we stopped to check, it was clear that it had been like that for a while. My medic and a couple of Soldiers went to work and saved this kid's life. It was a great feeling to know my men still had that care for others after everything they had gone through.

Again in Mosul, we would go outside the city to an Iraqi Army camp. On one of our routes to get there, a young boy would run out and wave with excitement in his eyes. He lived in a small hut about the size of a car and was always naked. After seeing him a couple of times we stopped, and I gave him one of my t-shirts. It was like a dress on him, and we gave out some candy and other items to him and the other kids around. I have never seen anyone so happy to have a t-shirt or anything else in my life. It is truly the best gift I have ever given to anyone.

I am so thankful to remember these moments. It reminds me that the American war fighter can be that war fighting machine or a compassionate and caring soul during all of that chaos. I think of those complaints and wants of people who seem to never have enough, and I just think, be thankful for what you have, because you could be praying to just have a t-shirt.

Redeployment by Warren Dupree

Reveille at 0600, roll out, cleanup dress blues, with spit-shined low quarters.
White hat, the white of a snowflake.
Took my last meal, and said my good-byes.
Muster on station, one last time.
More sadness on friends lost, never to be seen again.
Taking a last look at a past life.
I move to the ship's quarterdeck.
Standing on deck I hear the word passed, attention to colors, eight bells.
"Now hear this. Commence ship's work."
The daily routine begins.
With sea bag and orders in hand, the office of the watch logs me out.
Permission given to leave the ship.
I salute the colors and walk the gangway.
Once on the pier, I look to the future.
My work is done, duty completed.
Freedom, oh sweet freedom.

Left Right Boom Step by Theron Russell

Left right boom step, left right boom step! How did I get here? Left right boom step! I am just an aviation electrician. Left right boom step! Ok that is not technically true, I am a Marine and every marine is a rifleman. Left right boom step! But one week ago, hell two hours ago, I would not have thought I would be here. But here I am. Isn't it crazy how plans change?

Left right boom step! One week ago was Good Friday. I never understood why they called it that if it represents such a bloody horrific day. Left right boom step! Anyway, that is not the point; the point is that on good Friday, I had a plan, and this was not that plan. I was going to grandma's house in Georgia. My vehicle had been inspected, I'd filled out my chit to go out of bounds for liberty. I was ready to go when we were released at twelve hundred.

Left right boom step! Only four hours to go, no work on the bench, this day was dragging ooooon... "Russell, I need you in my office now." The gunny did not sound mad, but this was urgent.

"Aye, Aye Gunny." I replied and quick-timed it there.

Left right boom step!

"Go to your barracks, get your seven-eighty-two gear on your rack so I can inspect it," the green-eyed gunny said.

"Aye Aye gunnery sergeant," I replied, *oh shit, did I call him Gunny earlier?* He does not like to be called gunny! He didn't say anything, so I guess it is okay. I quickly got out of there.

Back in my room with everything laid out, having no idea why. "You are good to go Lance Corporal, now pack a C-bag, then go to the armory and check out your rifle. Make sure you are at the Parade Deck by twelve hundred," he said, in what seemed like one breath. "Oh, and call your grandmother and tell her you will not be there for Easter." And he walked out the door of the barracks. Left right boom step!

I made it to the Parade Deck by 1140, five minutes early. I found a place in line, and I started asking questions. I wanted, no, *I needed* answers. I was scared, concerned, and even a little excited. But not knowing, that was the hard part. I found my comfortable position on my C-bag with my other gear around me, holding my rifle. I sat and waited, and waited, then I waited some more. Left right boom step!

They loaded us on a bus and drove away and none of us knew why or where. Not even the NCO's seemed to have a clue. We knew we were driving north. Left right boom step! We arrived in Norfolk, Virginia, and we were told to take our gear onto the USS Bataan which is a Landing Helicopter Dock (LHD), a smaller aircraft carrier for helicopters. We went aboard, stowed our gear, and waited, and waited, then waited some more. Left right boom step!

At this point we were guessing the possibilities. Watching the news, the consensus was we were going to Cuba, because some kid who was the sole survivor from a rafting trip from Cuba to Miami was being sent back to family in Cuba since they had requested his return. The U.S. government had decided to honor the family's request which had become a big issue at the time. There were protests and threats against those who would be taking him back, so we were pretty sure we were going to be their escort back to Cuba. Left right boom step!

So, here I am on a boat in the middle of the ocean with no clue where I am going. We are practicing riot maneuvers. First and second squad carrying shields and batons. As cadence is called, left, right they would hit their shield, boom. I would jump and remind myself to step. Commands were called and the first squad would drop to a knee with their shields in front of them covering them from the ground up. Second squad would bring their shields over covering from the top of first squads shields and up. The rifle men would fill in the gaps and move around according to commands. It was like something you would see in Viking movies. We trained this way for days not knowing where we were going.

Then we found out, we were headed to Vieques, Puerto Rico. We were chasing people out of their homes to reclaim the property to make it a bombing range once again. Protestors from around the world came, including Ricky Martin. It is weird to me that just over a week ago I was making plans to go home and see my grandma and now I am here to chase someone's grandma from her home and this sound is stuck in my head, left right boom step!

I Did Not Know Your Name by Pete Ramsey

I did not know your name as I watch the Armored Personnel Carrier after having struck the landmine, pirouette like a Blue whale breaching the ocean's surface. To this day I see you hanging there in the hatch while your tether to life itself is being cut asunder, Bernard James Henry.

I did not know your names as I drive past the blast site which is within sight of the gate of Lai Khe and a modicum of safety. You were at the end of a year's tour duty in Vietnam. So close you were to seeing the faces of those you loved and who loved you. You were like lost souls caught in a blizzard for days on end who finally get to safety only to be snatched away by the Wolf of War as your hand makes contact with the doorknob. Added to the macabre twist of fate, all of you from the same town in New Hampshire: Guy Blanchette, Gaeton Beaudoin, Richard Genest, Richard Raymond and Robert Robichaud.

There are three body bags as well lying beside the road waiting to be picked up. They contain the remains of the unfortunate Vietnamese father, mother and daughter killed as well, I will never know your names. Your sin was just being alongside the stricken truck. I note the ruthlessness of warfare which can befall the innocent.

I did not know your names at the unexpected sound of an explosion shaking the air inside FSB Thunder 1. I sit in the mess tent eating along with several others. We only give it a passing thought. Shortly I will know the truth that death stalks you without pity once war has you in its talons. There is not an ounce of safety anywhere here. In a nightmarish turn of events, each step so simple and inane, but when put together they produce a lethal result. My troop Capt. John Howard Guthridge and SSG Charles Joseph Mac Donald have both been lost. Followed of course by the absurd mental gibberish of "Oh, I guess it was just their time" in an attempt to describe the indescribable.

I did not know your name as my Lieutenant walks back towards our APC with a shaken and ashen look on his face. On the right side of his forehead is a trickle of blood. He witnessed your passing. One account says it was a booby trap grenade while another account says something else. Whatever the cause, suddenly you were gone, Robert Benoit.

I did not know your name but am witness to the plume of black smoke and sound of screeching shrapnel. There is only a fragment of you left to be placed on the Dustoff. That morning you had sat on the APC as the orders of the day were being outlined for your ARVN counterparts. The look on your face had a faraway appearance and it still does today when I gaze over photos of the time. Helping train the ARVN soldier who at times seemed totally disinterested was a high-risk venture and you did so without regard for yourself, David Edward Kuczynski.

I did not know your name but only hear of your passing via the radio head set I am wearing. Your job is the same as mine, driver of an APC and thus the most vulnerable to immediate death from landmines. Having seen before the results of such an encounter I can only hope yours was an immediate departure with no suffering, Andrew B. Sexton.

I did not know your name as I looked at what remained of the APC you have been driving. Once again, we share a kinship of sorts in both being drivers. I did not know your name, but in the intervening hours, between seeing and hearing about your fate, we achieved a brotherhood and bond still holding strong today. The stark reality before me leaves no doubts in my mind as to the consequences of missing any hint or scent of immediate danger. You taught me to take nothing for granted and never ever let my thoughts stray. If I wanted to stay alive that is, Eugene Ray Jenkins.

I did not know your names as we secure the crash site of your small helicopter. The rotor blades are draped in a blackened and melted arch like a hideous crown over the disposition of your remains.

Both of you had just been awarded the Silver Star for sitting your craft right into the middle of a firefight to deliver plasma to badly wounded troops. Heroic and selfless yes, but fate had other plans for Henry J. Vad and James L. Downing.

I did not know your name but knew some who served with you. Someone higher up had thought that the cavalry would be a good place to mimic a television show back home called *The Rat Patrol*. What has happened instead? Despite your efforts and good leadership, the fragility of your transport and the quick ingenuity of the enemy has brought a swift end to an officer's Hollywood romances of glory. You bring a fantasy back to reality much, much too expensively, Burton K. Phillips.

I did not know your names as I drive you back into the village square. Your cadavers are piled up like discarded rag dolls in a makeshift bin on the front of my tank. Some of your faces are only a couple of feet from my own. Is my indifference a sign of lost humanity or a self-protection mechanism? Once dumped maybe the villagers will know of you. You are their problem now.

I did not know your names as I look over your bullet-riddled bodies. I did not know the names of your possible husbands or lovers. Maybe there are children somewhere waiting for your return. A mother or father wondering what has become of their girl child.

I did not know your names as you climb on board my track for an American-Vietnamese joint operation. I see small impish people who seem to be somewhat lackadaisical about what awaits in the day ahead. I watch you march off with the same attitude. Some with rifles up over their shoulders carried like afterthoughts. Some stroll like school kids holding each other's hand. I know that some of you will not see the day's end. I did not know your names, but I do remember your faces.

I did not know your name as I scream *NO!* at the Vietnamese medic about to inject you with a dose of morphine. You have sucking chest wounds and morphine will act like a lethal injection. He does anyway and my effort to get you to my stretcher has been for naught along with the risk I took getting to you.

I did not know all of your names as we split company on the eve of a fateful day. Voices and call signs will be the only tools of identification the next day as terror and desperation reigns supreme around you. By terror's end, and in the following days, I will come to know of Eldon Moore, Daniel L. Flynn, Everette L. Ankrom, Edward E Howard, William Bond and Jay W. King. And Billy Joe Schaffer, I knew your name only too well. We were brothers in arms at the very first handshake.

So what can be said then of the named and unnamed? Simply this. With absolute certainty, whether friend or foe, each embraced the desire to live and laugh with the same passion and joy as any one of us living today. Also like us, each asking of life, to please remember my name.

Cold in the Heat of War by Mike Sitman

Heat was always a dense factor.
Sweat dripping, relief never in sight.
Water was not enough of a detractor,
nor shade from the heat of sunlight.

But this was only a side note
from what things could become.
When waiting at your post
for the inevitable to come.

A lashing out of disparaging cries
as clashing soldiers begin to mass.
Disorienting sound from guns fly
from the engaging whiz of brass.

Will someone die here today?
Will it be me in the fray?
Or will it be them or they
for the beginning of decay.

Then, with total unbelief
your friend goes down.
I find my mouth is unable to speak
I breath in so not to drown.

When it is all over
giving inspection to the cold body,
I stare giving full exposure
no movement from his body.

The scene taps on my window
with the same amount of pain
seeing his face, even though it's been so
many years ago, the feelings still the same.

Home for the Holidays by Mike Smith

When old men sit in comfortable offices and choose war, they create an opportunity for the few to survive Saint Crispin's Day once again. Those of us who survive that Day want nothing more than peace.

. . .

She stood back a little, looking out the glass doors of the brightly-lit entrance to the gymnasium. The crowd bustled through the doors and around her, making way as they passed. All the soldiers carried the Screamin' Eagle patch on the sleeves of their uniforms—101st Airborne —as did she. The National Guard's 784th Transportation Battalion (Motor Support) had made it home in time for Thanksgiving and Christmas. Her fellow soldiers deferred to her as they passed.

I watched her. With other soldiers streaming through the door holding civilian loved ones, carrying children, gripping bouquets of red and yellow roses, she let them flow around her and looked at something far away. She stood apart in the midst of her battalion.

I waited for the crowd to thin and stepped to where I could see from behind her. Arms folded, she scanned left and right. I knew then. She had placed herself on overwatch. She had not been assigned; she had simply volunteered. With her battalion mustering in the gymnasium, she had positioned herself to see the perimeter. Even from behind, I knew exactly what her eyes scanned. They looked at buildings; they watched for movement on rooftops. Her eyes searched with the crystal clarity and complete concentration that only come from staying alive.

Here, I thought, *here is one of the wounded.*

Her digitally camouflaged uniform and desert boots were clean, straight. My black leather, chains, boots, and patched vest were not. Still, I walked up to her left and even with her, making sure I stayed a couple of paces away. I stood square to the glass doors, folded my arms, and began to scan with her. Then I said, "Are you gonna make muster?"

She continued scanning. "No."

"Perimeter's secure. I have your six. Grab a drink, soldier."

She checked my stance. She watched my eyes, and I didn't let them break away from the skyline. She approved me for perimeter watch and headed for the drinking fountain beside the main doors. I stayed put until she made it to the fountain; then I followed her.

I stood behind her until she finished her drink. She looked back at the exact spot she had left, and I said, "We're home now. Detail secure. … You did some hard things over there."

"Huh?"

I shook her hand. "Welcome home, soldier. I just know it must have been tough. It seems to me you saw action."

She looked at my motorcycle vest and the patches that said Vietnam Veteran. "It wasn't as tough as your war."

I smiled, "How often did you come under fire?"

"Every time we went out."

I could see there was more. Carrying our own shadows, we recognize them in others.

"What you did was as tough as anything we did in Vietnam. Don't let anyone tell you different."

Her eyes dropped.

"Soldier," I said. She looked back up.

"I heard a World War II vet say they take the same mud and move it from war to war – what he meant was there's no difference. War is just war."

"I guess."

"Kinda hard to tell who the enemy was?"

"Yeah." She was silent then. Whatever it was, it wanted to come out now. I had hit the nerve.

When she spoke again, she just stated it flatly. It was the only way she could.

"They tried to stop us. I was lead truck." Again she paused, and I just waited until she spoke again. "They would throw children in front of you and make you stop, then take you under fire."

Her expression did not change at all, and the horror behind it filled the space between us. And I knew.

I said it quietly for her then, the thing she wouldn't even whisper to herself. The quiet words, now outside, fell between us into the horror, into the bright lights inside the glass doors with the hard concrete floor in the entryway, where you looked outside and made sure, where you looked with clarity and saw the slightest movement on the far rooflines, where I used to look at a tree line the same way, where she and I stood with neither of us really there, and we weren't in the entryway, we weren't standing on a concrete floor with lights and glass doors; we were both in the other place, together and half a world away in the crushing sadness that neither of us wanted to bring into these bright lights on this smooth concrete behind these glass doors.

And she nodded yes. Damn. She nodded yes.

When a soldier swears that Christ is on a crutch and God is looking the other way, people think it's an exaggeration. Not always. Not this time.

"Soldier."

She looked up at me again, and I said, "You're a good troop ... I don't know how else to say it, probably because I'm an old fart who never saw women in combat, but you've earned your way into a brotherhood. When I call you Brother, I want you to know I mean you'll always be in my heart."

I shook her hand again, this time rolling up to lace our thumbs, palms together. I pulled her gently into the bear hug, the hug that tells us we are soldiers alive in the midst of things we have put away because they are too hard, because they cannot be known, because they cannot be spoken but must be said. I felt the bill of her uniform cap push sideways as it pressed on the leather of my vest against my heart. I felt the strength of her arm returning the hug and knew she understood the love that brought me into her darkness where we stood on the concrete floor in the bright lights where it is not safe but where we are together because our brotherhood dictates we stand together, because love must ultimately be stronger than all of it. I held her and waited because the hug was hers, not mine, and I let her hold it until she knew and let go.

Again she nodded; it was all she could do at the time. She straightened her cap and headed toward the ceremony. She would make muster after all. As she walked away, I remembered something.

"Hey, Soldier!"

She stopped and looked back. I snapped a salute. She came to attention and returned it. I saw a single tear on her face as she turned away. One salty tear.

The single tear was all just then. The rest of them, though, stand a chance of coming out someday, somehow. She might spend months, years, or a lifetime holding them back, but it is possible. In a safe and quiet life, with love around her, she might be able to free another tear. Then another. I can only pray that God will send her a veteran to listen if the time ever comes for all the tears at once.

On her day, the day the tears come, she might remember the time I said it for her. She might remember an older veteran who spoke the words; she might gather all strength; she might have enough strength to say it herself.

She was at the beginning, starting to live the life I had lived. If I could, I'd carry her through those tears. I would listen as she told of the sound of bullets clanging off steel, listen as she recalled unmarked open roads that explode, and I would hold her when she said it the first time.

She'll need to find a safe place to say it aloud, find the right ears to say it to, find a place where tears that seem they'll never stop can begin to flow. There, she can whisper her horror for the first time.

She kept her foot on the gas.

The Wall by Bruce Turek

It was a breezy, wet, cold day in DC at the wall, on a Friday
in October, 1990; the clouds were dark and low.
On that day, in front of the wall, I knelt sobbing, one knee on the
ground,
and one knee high, arm outstretched and fingers on his name, tracing
each letter.
I didn't know Steve well, this soldier, this fellow poker-player at night.

He would come back from a mission wet and totally exhausted, in need
of rest.
One afternoon, at lunch time, in 1967, he returned to base camp
at Pleiku, Central Highlands, with sores covering his entire body.
At the time, we didn't know about Agent Orange,
but we now know that he had been in the bush
where the defoliant had been sprayed.

He would come back to camp often, each time with more sores than
the last
and each night when he was back, sores upon sores, he would play
poker.

Then one night, he was not there even when his platoon had returned.
His sergeant said that he had been sent to Tay Ninh, to a hospital.

After 23 years, I would remember him, at the wall.
I would recall him, his laugh, his card playing;
remember him by tracing my fingers across his name on the black shiny
marble.

Then, unexpectedly, a hand was on my shoulder there at the wall, in
front of the names
etched into eternity. The stranger asked if I would talk.
I turned, answered and together we shuffled to a bench, there at the
wall.

The stranger's brother had served and been killed over there in the war
in that same platoon.
How had he found me? We comforted each other, there at the wall
on that cold, breezy, wet day, recalling and dignifying those of us
who had not returned.

We parted ways, the stranger and I, leaving behind that wall and each
other,
knowing that we had done for each other what no one else could have
done at the time;
we gave each other and our fallen friends and kin the tribute we all
deserve:

Memory, Honor and Respect.

Glossary of Terms

Afghanistan bases:

KAF: Kandahar Airfield.
BAF: Bagram Airfield.

Agent Orange: Agent Orange was an herbicide and defoliant the US used in Vietnam as part of its herbicidal warfare. Its name derives from the orange barrels that it was shipped in.

ARVN: Army of the Republic of Vietnam.

C-ration: Individually canned, prepackaged meals.

Chinook: The Boeing CH-47 Chinook is an American twin engine, tandem rotor heavy lift helicopter.

Cobra: The Bell AH-1 Cobra is a two bladed, single engine attack helicopter manufactured by Bell Helicopter.

Concertina Wire: A type of barbed wire or razor wire that is formed in large coils which can be expanded like a concertina.

Claymore: The M18A1 Claymore is a directional anti-personnel mine. The Claymore is command-detonated and directional, meaning it is fired by remote control and shoots a pattern of metal balls into the kill zone like a shotgun.

DMZ: Demilitarized Zone.

FOB: In Iraq, Forward Operating Bases. Bases or outposts or camps.

HO Chi Minh Sandals: A form of sandal in Vietnam made from re-cycled tires, distinctive of Vietnamese soldiers. Called "Ho Chi Minh Sandals" by Americans.

IED: Improvised Explosive Device, a bomb constructed and deployed in ways other than conventional military action.

KIA: Killed in Action.

Klicks: Kilometers.

LRRP: Long range reconnaissance patrol, a small, heavily armed reconnaissance team that patrols deep in enemy territory.

LZ: Landing Zone.

M-16: The M-16 rifle, officially designated Rifle, Caliber 5.56 mm, M16, is a United States military adaptation of the Armalite AR-15 rifle. In 1964, the M-16 entered military service and was deployed for jungle warfare in 1965 for Vietnam.

MP: Military Police.

NVA: North Vietnamese Army.

OP: Observation Post.

POW: Prisoner of War.

Slicks: Helicopters used to carry troops or cargo with only self-protective armaments.

SOF: Special Operations Forces.

Tet: January holiday, Buddhist lunar New Year. Buddha's birthday.

Tet Offensive: On January 31, 1968, 70,000 North Vietnamese and Viet Cong launched the TET offensive against South Vietnamese villages, cities, and military bases. It was a turning point for the war.

VC: Viet Cong. officially the National Liberation Front for South Vietnam, was an armed communist revolutionary organization in South Vietnam, Laos and Cambodia. It fought under the direction of North Vietnam, against the South Vietnamese and United States governments during the Vietnam War, eventually emerging on the winning side. It had both guerrilla and regular army units, as well as a network of cadres who organized peasants in the territory the Viet Cong controlled. During the war, communist fighters and anti-war activists claimed that the Viet Cong was an insurgency indigenous to the South, while the U.S. and South Vietnamese governments portrayed the group as a tool of North Vietnam. According to Tr'n Văn Trà, the Viet Cong's top commander, and the post-war Vietnamese government's official history, the Viet Cong followed orders from Hanoi and were part of the People's Army of Vietnam, or North Vietnamese army.

HKIA: Hamid Karzai International Airport where the last American solider left from.

Contributors

Alan Brett
Served in the US Army from 1966 to 1971. Served with 2nd. Of the 14th Infantry, 25th Infantry Division from 1967 to 1969, serving 35 months. In 1980 I became part of the VA's Vietnam Veterans Outreach Program in Wyoming as a therapist then in Colorado aa Team Leader. I joined the PTSD Clinical Team in Maryland as a therapist. Then started Trauma Services which encompassed an outpatient therapy program and a 12-week Residential Intensive PTSD Treatment Program, Retiring in 2011.

Allan Perkal
Weaverville, NC. United States Air Force. 26th Casualty Staging Flight. Vietnam 1967-1968.

Alton Whitley
Alton Whitley's 26 years in the Air Force included two tours in the Vietnam War flying the F-100 Supersabre and the A-7D Corsair. He was the first operational pilot to fly the F-117A stealth fighter in 1982 and commanded the 37th Tactical Fighter Wing in Desert Storm, flying 19 combat missions in the F-117A.

Anne Adkins
My name is Anne Adkins and I am a Gold Star mother. We lost our wonderful son on May 3, 2007, in Iraq.

Charles Bruce Turek
US Air Force, Weather Observer, August, 1963 to July, 1967. I was never stationed for duty at an Air Force base, rather attached to the Army for four years at Fort Hood, Texas, Fort Stewart and Fort Gordon, Georgia and in Vietnam, to the 4th Infantry Division, the 101st Airborne and the 1st Air Cavalry as Combat Weather and

Recon. I saw combat with them and spent the entire year at many locations in the field either in a one man tent or in boots. Mine was an unusual assignment.

Daniel Anest

Daniel Anest, 36, served 10 years in the Marine Corps and is the father of an almost 4 year old son, Noah. Daniel discovered his love of writing while participating in Veterans Treatment Court, of which he will graduate in August.

David Rozelle

United States Army, C Company, 15th Medical; 1st Cavalry Division. Vietnam 1970 – 1971. Lives in Old Fort, NC.

Dean Little

Dean A. Little, PA-C was a Medic at the 95th Evacuation Hospital at DaNang and was intermittently on loan to the III MAF Cap Team in Hoa An, Vietnam from 8/69-8/70.
Mr. Little was a medical staff member for 30+ years at the Charles George V.A.Medical Center in Asheville, NC. (Married with two adult children and a grandson.)

Donna Culp

Served in the USAF from 1985 – 1992 as an Occupational Therapist treating active duty, retirees, and their families who had a wide variety of neurological, and physical disabilities. Experiencing history in the making, she served in Germany when the Berlin Wall came down, Desert Shield/Desert Storm, the reunification of Germany, and the beginning of the US military drawdown after the Soviet Union fell.

Dorian Dula

I moved to Western North Carolina in July of 2020. I Retired in March of 2020. I grew up in California and after the Marine Corps I graduated with my Undergraduate Degree from San Jose St. and later my MBA from Golden Gate Univ. in San Francisco.

Frank Cucumber
United States Army, 1969-1972, 815th Engineers, 18th Engineer
Brigade, Vietnam 1970.

Gabriel Garcia
Captain Gabriel Garcia, North Carolina National Guard. Served
in Afghanistan 2013-14 on Active Duty with the 82nd Airborne
Division. I currently live in Arden, NC.

Gerald Biggs
I joined the Air Force in 1960 served 20 plus years. Three years in
support of the Vietnam war and also one year in Vietnam. Retired
from the Air Force in 1980.

Gerry Nieters
Immediately after finishing my internship I was drafted and sent
to Fort Sam Houston for one month's orientation and then sent to
Vietnam. I was assigned to surgery at a 400 bed 36th Evacuation
Hospital in Vung Tau for six months I was then assigned to the 2nd
battalion 39th infantry brigade 9th Division as a battalion surgeon
for six months in the Mekong Delta. I DEROS'd Sept. 1968. After
residency training at Duke University in Diagnostic Radiology, I
practiced radiology in western North Carolina until retirement in
1998.

James Watts
United States Marine Corp, Charlie Company, 2nd Battalion, 3rd
Marine Division, Vietnam 1969-1970.

Jim Hugenschmidt
James Hugenschmidt carried an M-16 from September, 1968, to
September, 1969, as an infantry soldier with the 199th Light Infantry

Brigade based in Long Binh, III Corps, operating north and west of Saigon. In his two years of Army service he reached the rank of Staff Sergeant.

John Sitman
One of 4 brothers who served there at different times. I was the last to go. I was attached to the 101st AB Div. and then with their Medevac unit with several different units under that umbrella. My main unit was with the 44th Medical Brigade out of Bien Hoa, but stationed up on the DMZ.

Kevin Wierman
Navy 1981 - 1990 = Nuclear Power Propulsion Instructor, Engineering Laboratory Technician & earned Submarine Warfare Pin. Navy 2001 – 2008, earned SeaBee Combat Warfare Pin and transferred to Navy Inshore Boat Unit shortly after.

Michael White
I was born on 9/11, and joined the Army at the suggestion of a girlfriend. With high scores on my testing, I had a multitude of job choices, and wanted to pick something I could use when I got out, so I went with technology - radio retransmission operator. After time in combat, my nightmares were pretty bad and I suppressed those with substances. A buddy of mine said he thought I may have "shell shock" and I should go to the VA. I got into some serious trouble, but Kevin Rumley helped me find the Veterans Treatment Court and there hope for this paratrooper still yet.

Midge Lorence
Tom was part of the writing group called Brothers Like These, now called Brothers and Sisters Like These. He asked me one day, when he was scheduled to read for Veterans Day, if I would be able to go and do it for him, as he could not breathe. I was more than happy to go and help him fulfill his obligation. After Tom passed away in March of

2019, I was invited to stay with the group, and to read some of Tom's pieces. Iwas also encouraged to start writing some of my own pieces as well, and I can say without a doubt, it has helped tremendously with my healing process.

Mike Smith
Navy E4. Minesweeping and board-and-search operations at the DMZ and the Qua Viet River, 1969, 1970, 1971. Currently retired on ten acres in Heaven, which is just North of Asheville in Madison County.

Monica Blankenship
Monica Walsh Blankenship, (Mary Monica Walsh). RN, MSN, former Cpt, USAF - Active duty Air Force nurse at Travis AFB 1974-1976, active reserve Flight Nurse 1977-1981, Travis. Widowed, large family, residing, after many different homes, in Asheville NC. Active, volunteer work.

Pete Ramsey
I was born 1949 from the descendants of the early settlers of WNC and the New England states. Like so many of those men who served in the Nations Wars through the years, I too was an Infantryman. My war was Vietnam 1969-70.

Ray Crombe
Drafted in 1968, training in Fort Dix, Fort Polk, and Fort Benning. Then to Vietnam in the 1st Cavalry, Company E Recon, 2nd Battalion of the 7th Cav in 1969 and 1970. Sure wish I had been wiser and more mature during those years.

Renee Hermance
I was in the Marines. I served during Desert Storm. The Mediterranean and sea deployments. Heavy equipment operator.

Ron Kuebler

Retired engineer/speech pathologist and served as Infantry Sergeant(Intelligence) with HQ and D Company, 5/46th Infantry Regiment, 198th LIB, Americal Division at FSB Gator near Chu Lai Defence Center from 9/69-8/70. Wife: Margot(since 1973); three Eagle Scout sons: Scott, Gregory, Matthew.

Ron Toler
9th Special Operations Squadron, DaNang AB Vietnam 1971-72, 912th Air Refueling Squadron, Taiwan '72, Thailand '73, Okinawa, '73.

Stacie Litsenberger
Stacie Litsenberger is a retired Army Major. She continues to work as an Occupational Therapist at the CGVAMC and is a major supporter of Brothers and Sisters like These and Warrior Canine Connection.

Stephen Henderson
USMC, served in Quang Tri Province, I Corp in India Company 3/4 3rd Marine Division, 1969-70.

Ted Minnick
My name is Ted Minnick—I served in the US Army from 1966-2006. I was a Field Artillery Battery Commander with the 6th BN, 32d Field Artillery, IFFV in II Corps, Republic of Vietnam in 1969-1970. My battery consisted of 2-8in howitzers, 2-175mm guns, various gun trucks and other tracked vehicles.

Theron Russell
I am a veteran who served in the Marine Corps from 1999 to 2003. I was born and raised just outside of Flint, Michigan. I enjoy writing, painting, and playing music.

Tom Lorence
Tom was a Vietnam veteran, US Army, 25th Infantry, 1967 to 1968.
Those were the two deadliest years in that war. He was part of task
force 35 during the Tet offensive at Ton Son Nhut Air Force Base.
There were so many things he could not remember, just bits and pieces,
and would yell out occasionally when he had nightmares. He was
diagnosed with situational amnesia. He didn't die in that war, but sadly
he died from it in March of 2019.

Tommy Cannon
My name is Tommy Cannon. I am from the small North Carolina
town of Mills River. I joined the Army on September 5th of 2001. I
served nearly 14 years as an Infantry Soldier and deployed three times
to Iraq. I now live just a few miles from that small town I grew up
in with my amazing wife of 22 years and my two children. I am so
thankful for these Brothers and Sisters Like These who changed my life
and truly brought me home.

Warren Dupree
United States Navy, 1967-1973; United States Coast Guard, 1977-
1979; North Carolina Army National Guard, 1979-2009. Vietnam
1968-1969; Desert Shield/Desert Storm 1990-1991.

Made in the USA
Columbia, SC
23 January 2023

10089612R00112